# Am I My Planet's Keeper?

Global Warming. Climate Change. Climate Crisis. Climate Emergency. Whatever label we use, we are facing one of the greatest challenges to the survival of life as we know it.

But while addressing greenhouse gases is perhaps our most urgent need, it's not our only task. We must also address toxic waste, pollution, habitat destruction, and our other contributions to the world's sixth mass extinction event.

To do that, we must simultaneously address the unmet human needs that keep us distracted from deeper engagement in stabilizing our climate: economic inequality, universal healthcare, tuition-free college and vocational training, fare-free public transit, and subsidized childcare.

And to accomplish *that*, we must unite to combat the monied forces that use fear, prejudice, and misinformation to manipulate us.

It's a daunting task. But success is our only option.

# Praise for Johnny Townsend

In *Zombies for Jesus*, "Townsend isn't writing satire, but deeply emotional and revealing portraits of people who are, with a few exceptions, quite lovable."

Kel Munger, *Sacramento News and Review*

In *Sex among the Saints,* "Townsend writes with a deadpan wit and a supple, realistic prose that's full of psychological empathy….he takes his protagonists' moral struggles seriously and invests them with real emotional resonance."

Kirkus Reviews

*Inferno in the French Quarter: The UpStairs Lounge Fire* is "a gripping account of all the horrors that transpired that night, as well as a respectful remembrance of the victims."

Terry Firma, Patheos

"Johnny Townsend's 'Partying with St. Roch' [in the anthology *Latter-Gay Saints*] tells a beautiful, haunting tale."

Kent Brintnall, Out in Print: Queer Book Reviews

*Selling the City of Enoch* is "sharply intelligent...pleasingly complex...The stories are full of...doubters, but there's no vindictiveness in these pages; the characters continuously poke holes in Mormonism's more extravagant absurdities, but they take very little pleasure in doing so....Many of Townsend's stories...have a provocative edge to them, but this [book] displays a great deal of insight as well...a playful, biting and surprisingly warm collection."

Kirkus Reviews

*Gayrabian Nights* is "an allegorical tour de force...a hard-core emotional punch."

Gay. Guy. Reading and Friends

*The Washing of Brains* has "A lovely writing style, and each story [is] full of unique, engaging characters....immensely entertaining."

Rainbow Awards

In *Dead Mankind Walking*, "Townsend writes in an energetic prose that balances crankiness and humor....A rambunctious volume of short, well-crafted essays..."

Kirkus Reviews

I0542605

# Am I
# My Planet's
# Keeper?

## Cooperating in the Midst of a Mass Extinction

## Johnny Townsend

*Am I My Planet's Keeper?*

# Contents

*Johnny Townsend*

# Repetition Is the Greatest Teacher

When we talk about global warming, those on the left are often afraid of doing it the wrong way. We worry the term "global warming" has lost its meaning, so we start saying "climate change" instead. Then we move on to "climate crisis." That starts to feel weak after a while, so we try out "climate emergency." And then "climate breakdown."

There's nothing inherently wrong with this approach. But sometimes, I fear those on the left try too hard to be different and original. Those on the right have perfected repetition as a powerful tool. It annoys the rest of us, *but it works*.

If you say "fake news" seven thousand times, people believe it. If you use "woke" in a pejorative way eight thousand times, even those who used to feel it a great descriptor start feeling defensive. If you say an election was "stolen" nine thousand times, you get people riled up enough to riot. If you call people "groomers" ten thousand times, you get people to start making laws against those you've targeted.

Folks in AA hear the same messages week after week, year after year. Repetition is a good teacher.

As a writer, I'm afraid of repetition. I don't want my work to sound monotonous. I don't want a new piece to sound like "old material."

So you'll find in this collection a mix of approaches. I simply can't resist trying new approaches to persuade people to action, yet the message is pretty much the same every time. We're in a crisis and must do something, anything we can think of, to start addressing the problem immediately, not ten or twenty or thirty years from now.

And the only way we can do that successfully is if we also address the multiple other issues holding people back. Some of those obstacles include various aspects of human nature but most are the direct result of capitalism, which puts profit, often short-term profit, above everything else.

Because those on the right have successfully vilified socialism by repeating misinformation and because those on the right, as well as corporate Democrats and most religious leaders we may have known growing up, have repeatedly championed capitalism as "God's economic policy," it's difficult for us to escape all that repetition.

We must get over both our indoctrination and our fears if we want any chance at mitigating the catastrophic changes ahead. Tipping points aren't reversible.

And I'll say so in these pages, over and over again. Hopefully, some of these essays will speak to you personally. I also hope you'll find pieces you think will speak to your friends and family who still need a push to accept reality.

Please, consider writing some op-eds and letters to the editor yourself. Or working in a field that allows you many hours a week finding solutions. And doing anything else you think might help.

# Treating a Critically Ill Climate

Virtually all moderate Democratic politicians accept donations from fossil fuel corporations. Then they seem, oddly enough, to have a difficult time voting for a ban on fracking or new oil pipelines. We "need" fossil fuels until "someone" develops renewables to an extent allowing us to "gradually" switch over. We can't do anything drastic that would disturb the economy. We must be "smart."

If someone had a case of bacterial meningitis, though, they wouldn't say, "You know, I have a big presentation coming up in a few weeks. I'm too busy right now preparing for it. And the deal will fall through completely if I'm not there to handle this. I won't get that promotion I've been working for. I'll just take a couple of vitamins and power through until a more convenient time to address this life-or-death illness."

If someone is diagnosed with melanoma, they wouldn't say, "I suppose this might be serious, if you want to be melodramatic about it. But I've been planning that trip to the beach for months. It would really disappoint the kids if we didn't go. I'll just start drinking some orange juice now and worry about setting an appointment with the oncologist when we get back."

To be fair, some people *do* make these kinds of decisions. But I think the medical literature will show things don't usually turn out well for them. And to be fair, all too often things don't turn out so good even for those who *are* sensible enough to take immediate action.

But at least they stand a chance.

When my husband developed liver cancer, he was devastated. He wanted to start chemotherapy right away. But the doctor said there was no chemotherapy for his type of cancer. My husband wanted radiation treatment. But the doctor said there was no radiation treatment for his type of cancer. My husband wanted surgery. But the doctor said that because of the location of the tumor, there was no surgery for his type of cancer. My husband wanted a liver transplant. But the doctor said he wasn't a good candidate to be added to the waiting list.

"Why won't they help me?" he asked me over and over in despair.

My husband died three months after his diagnosis without ever having undergone any treatment at all. To be sure, treatment would have been devastating to our personal "economy." But you know what? So was his dying. Losing the house was the smallest of my problems as the one left behind.

It's quite possible the climate is too ill for us to be able to cure it. And it's likely that some portion of the human species will survive the calamities coming our way in any event, even if billions die. Maybe trying to slow down and reverse global warming is like a deluded patient taking snake oil to cure their ALS. We're just kidding ourselves to think there's anything we can do.

But unless we're ready to accept that our fate is the complete eradication of life as we know it, we need to do more than say, "Our goal is to reduce carbon emissions 40% by the year 2050." Our cancer will be Stage 4 by then.

I understand that denial is a real, psychological reaction to devastating news. But if we want to survive, we need to get some counseling, deal with reality, and start our treatment. Someone who weighs 400 pounds isn't going to return to a healthy weight by making one extra lap to the mailbox and back.

It's time for *drastic* action on climate if we are to save ourselves.

# Superstition Is Leading Us Toward Extinction

Humans are an intelligent, rational species. We build upon existing knowledge to understand ourselves and the world around us. This trait has allowed us to overcome almost every obstacle and reign as the dominant species on the planet. So why haven't we been able to incorporate the science around greenhouse gases into our collective consciousness and adjust our behavior accordingly?

In addition to being highly rational creatures, it seems, we're also highly irrational.

Smart, intelligent people will throw a pinch of salt over their shoulder. We'll avoid walking under a ladder, change direction if a black cat crosses our path. We worry that if we break a mirror, we'll have seven years bad luck. We believe in Santa Claus and the Tooth Fairy.

Sure, we grow out of many superstitious beliefs over time, but not all of them. Most of the adults in my life still say "Knock on wood" so as not to tempt Fate. I see adults cross their fingers, make the sign of the cross, don their lucky shirt. They play the lottery using their lucky numbers, repeat unique rituals before a game or a job interview.

We watch "Charmed" and "Touched by an Angel" and every Harry Potter movie because part of us not only *hopes* there's something greater out there but also *believes* on some level that magic and the supernatural are real forces, if we can only tap into them.

Many of my Mormon friends and family don't feel the need to act on climate change because they believe Jesus will return any day now and take care of everything.

These are people who wear magic underwear every day of their adult lives.

I mean no disrespect. I used to wear them, too. I still keep a pair, thirty years after being excommunicated.

My previous partner taught at a religious university. An avowed atheist, Tom still maintained his fair share of superstitions. When he was diagnosed with liver cancer, I saw first-hand how humans cling to irrationality like a life preserver. Tom refused to write a will out of fear that doing so would jinx him.

Of course, superstition is not an effective treatment against biology, and he was dead three months later. His superstition had real-life consequences, however, if not for him, then for those around him. Since gay marriage wasn't legal at the time, Tom's estranged sister was legally his next of kin and inherited the house, his pension, his CDs in the bank, and everything else.

Perhaps our refusal to act on climate change won't affect us personally very much, but it will certainly affect the billions of others left here after we die. Are our grandchildren spoiled brats, selfish for wanting to inherit a habitable world?

As a Mormon missionary in Rome, I was instructed not to dust my feet off on anyone, no matter how provoked I might be. Dusting our feet was a ritual so powerful even God couldn't refuse to act on it and would be bound to afflict whoever we'd cursed.

As elders in the LDS Church, we held the priesthood, a mystical power that would allow us to heal the sick. My missionary companion and I blessed a member of our congregation in Sardinia, promising him a full recovery.

He was dead the next day.

My companion and I "knew" that if we'd only been more righteous, the man would have lived.

If faith or priesthood or other magical powers can only function on occasion, in a few isolated cases, when we're exceptionally devoted, then relying on those as our primary tools to solve an existential crisis is not a solid plan.

Mormons are told to pray as if everything depends on God but act as if everything depends on us.

Maybe the Messiah is coming back...and maybe he isn't. What's clear, though, is that it's up to us, through real, concrete, scientific measures, to take drastic action and transform our civilization to something sustainable.

Giving climate scientists and activists the Evil Eye is not good policy. So let's use the brains evolution gave us, put aside our superstitions, and act as if the world is real, with the belief—no, the knowledge—that reality matters.

# Can We Stop the Asteroid Heading for Earth?

When I heard the TED talk Greta Thunberg gave in Stockholm, I was impressed with the clarity of her vision. The Swedish high school student is leading student strikes and protests in Europe to force immediate action on climate change. Greta has Asperger syndrome, which makes her see issues in black and white. If the world is really in such imminent danger, she asked herself, why are we going about our lives as normal?

During WWII, the Allies accepted rationing and the draft and injury and death to protect our families and save our way of life. Greta was mystified at our inaction now over an existential crisis even greater. What in the world was wrong with us?

We don't have to be on the autism spectrum ourselves to realize she's absolutely right.

In the movie *Armageddon*, Bruce Willis plays a deep-sea oil driller who is sent with a team into space to prevent an asteroid from hitting the Earth. There's no time to waste. Every imaginable resource is directed into the effort to save humanity.

Spoiler alert: Even with everyone working together, they are only able to minimize the disaster, not avoid it altogether.

Likewise, the choice we face in real life is between minimizing climate disaster down to "moderate" devastation or allowing it to wreak unimpeded havoc across the globe.

Placing my recyclables in the right bin, while important, isn't going to prevent that asteroid from striking the planet. Convincing another 5% of the population to give up meat and dairy isn't going to do the trick, either.

If we banned Agent Orange and asbestos and lead because of the danger they presented, then why can't we ban or at least limit beef and other husbandry and agricultural products that create so much of the danger we face now?

Greta Thunberg concluded her TED talk by expressing how tired she is of people ending what little discussion exists on reducing carbon emissions by offering hope. We don't need hope, she said. We need action.

If we've used up our sick leave at work and then wake up one morning with shortness of breath and chest pain, do we go to work to avoid a reprimand and the loss of a day's pay? Or do we head to the hospital?

If we only have a part-time job and no health insurance, what do we do when our five-year-old pulls a pot of boiling spaghetti sauce off the stove and is badly burned? Do we simply decide we don't have enough money for a visit to the ER, much less her extended treatment? Or do we address the disaster at hand and worry about the bill later, even knowing it will burden us for years?

Going on as if nothing extraordinary is happening is pathologically inappropriate. We might even say such behavior constitutes mental illness.

What do we normally do when people are a danger to themselves and to others?

When my mother was hospitalized with leukemia at the age of forty-three, the family took shifts so that someone was always by her side. On the last day of my mother's life, I was scheduled to start my second shift after attending class on the other side of town.

I knew Mom's health was precarious when I relieved my father earlier that morning. She was still losing blood through her bowels. She'd experienced a stroke the day before that left her comatose, her left side paralyzed. I knew once I started that second shift, I'd probably be staying until the bitter end.

I could have gone directly to the hospital after class. But instead I went home to eat first. When I finally did arrive at the oncology unit, my sister met me in the hall. Mom had died five minutes earlier, with my sister, my dad, and my grandmother by her side.

I'd treated the day as if life was proceeding normally. I used to be proud I didn't miss my Geology exam earlier that afternoon. I was a trouper.

I would have been one of those in the South Tower who diligently stayed at my desk on 9/11 until it was too late. After all, it was the North Tower that was struck by a plane. There would still have been meetings to plan, finance reports to complete.

"The show must go on!" is a fine motto when performing a stage production, but we aren't actors in a play.

An asteroid is heading for the Earth. If we can't divert its path within the next twelve years, that rock six miles across is going to smash right into us. 80% of all life on Earth was wiped out the last time an asteroid this size struck the planet.

But we're not dinosaurs. We can do something about it.

Or, if changing our behavior is too difficult, we can sit back and daydream about which dominant life form might develop five or ten million years from now. We can fantasize about how they'll write books describing the fossilized bones they find all over the world belonging to a remarkable species that seemed to go extinct overnight.

They'll try to understand all that can be learned about our intelligence and behavior from bones and various artifacts, and they'll teach their children about how magnificent the Age of Humans must have been.

# One Million Elephants in Miami

Humans are an invasive species crowding out thousands of others and creating the first mass extinction event in the history of the planet *not* caused by meteorite impacts, supervolcanoes, or other natural disasters. Religious leaders must encourage their followers to have fewer children, and governments must create financial incentives for couples to voluntarily limit the number of children they bring into the world.

Those who don't understand science insist that even with 7.5 billion people, the Earth is not overpopulated, that there is room for billions more.

But what if we reverse the argument?

Today, the U.S. has a population of roughly 325 million people. What if we shared this space with 325 million grizzly bears? Or 325 million pythons? 325 million wolverines?

Ecosystems only thrive when the ratio of predator to prey can be sustained, so a country the size of the U.S. would never be able to accommodate that many large predators. Perhaps, then, mine isn't a realistic argument.

Except that humans are top predators worldwide, and we're wiping out more of the species below us every year.

Across the globe, there are approximately 3900 tigers of varying species. What would the world look like if there were 7.5 billion tigers filling up the continents?

That's 7,500,000,000.

The number is too staggering to comprehend. So let's narrow the focus. What would Puget Sound look like if 725,000 orcas filled the waters next to Seattle? How safe would we feel if 200,000 mountain lions walked the streets of Salt Lake City? Would we vacation in Pensacola if 52,000 alligators crawled along its beaches?

Are even those numbers too large to understand?

How about 2000 rhinos defecating on your child's high school playing field? 150 wolves jogging alongside you around the block? 15 cheetahs roaming about every Burger King? 5 jackals staring at you every time you walked into your back yard? 5 jackals in *everyone's* back yard—in your city, in every city in your state, across the country, and around the world?

Consider the relevance of needing to choose such tiny pinpoints on the map to even begin appreciating the impact of that many unwanted, dangerous bodies.

And then let's go back to more appropriate numbers. Could the residents of Mexico City compete with 8,850,000 jaguars? What would happen to the 9,275,000 inhabitants of Tokyo if 9,275,000 macaques moved in?

It's natural for us to want to propagate not only our own personal DNA but also that of our species. It's instinctive.

But we all know the story of the scorpion and the frog. It may well be in our nature to reproduce without restraint, but if we continue to do so, we'll all drown in a river filled with millions of other scorpions.

But not so many frogs. In the past couple of decades, over 200 of their species have already gone extinct.

# I'm Two Days Older Than You, So I'm Always Right

When children with the Sunrise Movement confronted Senator Dianne Feinstein over her inaction on climate change, reminding her of the report concluding we only had twelve years left to prevent irreversible destruction, she told them she'd been making policy for thirty years. "I know what I'm doing." She belittled the youth who came to ask her for protection. She was older than they were and clearly knew more. She couldn't be bothered with anything children might say.

In almost every sense of the word, someone Feinstein's age does in fact "know" more than a twelve-year-old or sixteen-year-old. How could they not? But just being old doesn't automatically make every opinion and position an older person holds correct. If that were the case, Trump would be right most of the time. He's certainly older than the majority of Americans.

Feinstein failed when she used her age and time on the job as proof she knew better than the people she was representing. If we don't want a government run by oligarchs, age isn't a much better qualification for leadership. In fact, when people dislike an older politician, it's often their age which is used as a weapon against them.

"Bernie Sanders is too old. Hillary Clinton is too old. Elizabeth Warren is too old." But if it's a "moderate" who doesn't want to accept scientific evidence, her age has taught *her* the wisdom of being "reasonable."

While I don't think Feinstein's age gives her ignorance of science the weight she thinks it does, I also don't think it counts against her. The problem is her position, not her age. "I have seven grandchildren," she said to the students who came to her office, as if that proves she would never do anything to harm the next generation. As if parents never kill their children. As if grandparents never molest their grandchildren. Having offspring is no proof of altruism or morality. If Feinstein *didn't* have children, would that mean we couldn't trust anything she said?

Trump has children, too, obviously. That hardly makes his position on mercury levels, water pollution, coal, or anything else right. How about his censoring climate change information from the EPA, the Energy Department, and the State Department websites?

When Feinstein was first elected as senator, she didn't vote only the way senior senators told her to. She didn't feel back then that their time on the job made every position they took the right one no matter what she believed personally.

Feinstein's age, her gender, her offspring, her skin color, her religious background, and the size of her shoes have nothing to do with the issues being discussed. Greenhouse gases, global warming, and climate change are dangers we can only address with scientific evidence and a massive, international effort to save what we can.

When elected officials refuse to support the Green New Deal because of donations from fossil fuel industries or an inability to wrap their heads around the science, they must be abandoned in favor of leaders willing to step up and face reality. We don't have four years or six years or eight years to slowly convince them of the need to act.

The DNC freely gives our money to candidates who protect the fossil fuel industry, so we can't give our donations to the Party, only to individual candidates and organizations that support essential policies. We only have a handful of election cycles left before it will simply be too late to do anything meaningful to limit the most devastating consequences of climate change.

Maybe that twelve-year-old who Feinstein dismissed as irrelevant doesn't know who Dan White is. But she knows something Feinstein doesn't, the urgency of the situation. The senator told the children she didn't like being given the ultimatum, "your way or the highway," stating stonily, "I don't respond to that." Feinstein then told the kids she was going to do what she wanted to do and if they didn't like it, that was too bad. The kids at least learned a lesson in double standards.

One wonders if she treats her seven grandchildren with the same W.C. Fields impersonation. "Go away, kid, you bother me." Sounds like a remake is in the works.

Of course, that's the way it is almost always with moderate Democrats. They want the rest of us to just accept whatever they say and do. Progressives, conservationists, scientists—we're just too stupid and naïve to understand how the real world works.

Maybe sixteen-year-olds can't vote, Senator. But there are plenty of voters over the age of eighteen who won't be dismissed as easily. We're tired of being treated like children by "wise," "reasonable" moderates. Democrats who refuse to do what's necessary on *any* of the essential issues won't have to wait twelve years to see their world falling apart. *That* political change is already here.

# Drawing a Line in the Tar Sands

Should we demand that our candidates refuse donations from fossil fuel corporations? Should we insist they commit to some form of a Green New Deal? Just as age or residency are minimum requirements for various positions, we must make a candidate's commitment to addressing climate change a prerequisite for any office.

In the Ravenna Park area of Seattle, a magnificent old-growth forest used to stand, with fir and cedar giants reaching 400 feet into the air, some trees measuring forty-four feet in circumference. Conflicting stories exist over the fate of the trees, which were all cut down by 1926. Some claim the Seattle Parks department logged them after dishonestly marking the trees as diseased. Others claim the local homeowners feared an increase in traffic as the trees grew in fame. Either way, one thing is clear—humans have a consistent history of committing monstrous environmental atrocities for the most mundane of reasons.

We saw this human impulse at work again with the thirty-five-day partial government shutdown in early 2019. The shutdown alone revealed the pettiness and greed of human nature, but the environmental impact created during a mere thirty-five days, the blink of an eye in ecological terms, was devastating. Without supervision, visitors to Joshua Tree National Park cut down normally protected 150-year-old trees. The park was damaged so seriously that officials estimated it would take hundreds of years for the area to recover. Hundreds of years to amend the sins of thirty-five days.

Even worse was what happened over in the Bureau of Land Management. Only "essential" workers were supposed to work during the shutdown, but the BLM determined that workers processing permits could pay their own salaries by approving pretty much every permit that came their way. So they approved a record 267 onshore drilling permits.

Many politicians, and the voters who elect them, have a vague sense that climate change is a problem, maybe even a serious one, but it exists for us on a theoretical level. Like worrying about paying for cosmetic surgery we've always wanted when we're struggling to pay this month's mortgage.

But Hurricane Sandy didn't happen in the future. Neither did Hurricane Katrina or Hurricanes Maria, Harvey, or Florence. Cyclone Idai didn't happen in the future. Or Typhoon Haiyan. Or the dozens of other increasingly devastating storms wreaking havoc around the globe.

The unprecedented flooding this year in the American Midwest didn't occur in the future. The destruction of Paradise last year by widespread California wildfires didn't occur in the future. The devastating Greek wildfires in 2018 and the cataclysmic Australian bushfires of 2009 didn't occur in the future. The 2010 heat wave that killed over 55,000 people in Russia didn't occur in the future.

These events may be "weather" rather than "climate," but weather and climate are not unrelated. The death and destruction and financial burden—in the billions, tens of billions, hundreds of billions of dollars—aren't abstract dangers for the future. They are our present.

The future will be worse.

All fossil fuel extraction is damaging to the local environment. All fossil fuel transportation, whether by train, truck, ship, or pipeline, is subject to catastrophic failure. All fossil fuel usage adds even more carbon to our environment.

We need to invest immediately in greener forms of energy and the infrastructure to support them. We must concentrate immediately on effective ways to extract carbon already in our air.

If we can't ban all fossil fuel extraction and usage overnight, we must, at the very least, demand our candidates reject all donations from fossil fuel corporations. We must demand that our elected officials no longer approve any new oil and gas development. We must draw a line in the tar sands. This far, and no farther.

# A Treatment Plan for Stage 3 Climate Cancer

When I spoke to my doctor a couple of days ago, I realized her approach to treating my Stage 3 cancer was exactly the same as the one our leaders are implementing to address the crisis of climate change.

During the latest visit with my oncologist, we went over her proposed treatment plan. "We'll start you on radiation immediately," Dr. Stewart said, "but even if you don't notice any effects right away, it's going to be hard on you, so we'll wait a bit before starting the chemotherapy."

I sighed. I'd watched my mother, both her parents, and my husband die of various cancers. "How long before we start the chemotherapy?" I asked.

"That depends." she replied. "We *could* start in four to six weeks. But I want to make sure your treatment is as painless as possible, so I recommend waiting a full six months after the last radiation treatment."

I frowned. "And how long will the chemotherapy take?"

Dr. Stewart shrugged. "Normally, it's just a couple of weeks. But that's so hard on patients. We'll go ahead and give you lower doses over a six-month period."

"Excuse me?"

"Most of my patients only feel minimal side effects on this schedule."

"But Dr. Stewart," I said, "I already looked up my cancer online. WebMD says most patients don't even live a full year after diagnosis without undergoing immediate, radical treatment."

She nodded with a bored expression, as if I were stating the obvious. "That's right. You're not going to live to finish your treatment."

"What?"

"I just think it's important not to act too drastically. Intensive therapy is hard work. It's expensive. You'll feel like crap. It's no fun. And you only have a 65% chance of survival even if we go all out."

Was I hearing this right? I felt like I was in the middle of a Kafka novel. "And if we follow your plan?"

"You'll be dead in a year, of course." She paused. "Well, you do have a 3% chance of spontaneous remission. You never know." She looked at her watch.

"But Dr. Stewart..."

"For Pete's sake," she huffed, "stop telling me how to do my job!"

Politicians don't want to pass legislation requiring the extreme, desperate measures we need to implement as a country and as a global community to limit the emission of additional greenhouse gases and convert to greener forms of energy.

It's too hard.

It's too expensive.

It's no fun.

There's no guarantee it will work anyway.

What we do know, though, is that *not* confronting the problem in a focused, aggressive way ensures with 100% certainty we'll fail.

I don't have cancer myself right now, but I have in fact watched loved ones die from various forms of the disease. And you know what?

My mother's death was hard.

My grandfather's death was expensive.

My grandmother's death was no fun.

My husband stayed in the denial stage until his very last day. The look on his face when he finally realized what was about to happen was one of the saddest moments of my life.

Not to mention his.

We don't have the luxury of allowing our political representatives to remain in denial. Industries which refuse to accept the reality of climate crisis, and politicians who are willingly manipulated by their big donors, are a cancer on the planet and the life on it, Stage 3 cancer fast approaching Stage 4.

We need to reverse the current triage procedure, bypassing politicians who won't develop a realistically urgent treatment plan, and devote our time, energy, and money to those who will at least give us a fighting chance.

# Bracing Ourselves for Climate Combat

We all know the stressful changes required to mitigate climate crisis. We understand the necessity of giving up oil and coal and natural gas. We know we must drastically cut meat consumption, divert tax money from the military budget into developing an entirely new infrastructure that can support renewable energy.

Adapting to such massive changes seems too awful to contemplate. So we simply pretend it isn't necessary and go about our lives as usual.

What happens when a diabetic decides that daily finger pricks, daily injections, and daily deprivations are just too much to ask and refuses to comply with the strict regimen?

Does their diabetes go away?

Precancerous polyps don't go away because we avoid colonoscopies, either.

The glaciers in Greenland won't miraculously stop melting if we refuse to listen to factual coverage of climate change.

It's important to remember we're capable of doing legitimately difficult things. In fact, most of us already have.

As Mormons, we make difficult adjustments throughout our lives. Many of us work for two years as full-time volunteer missionaries. We adjust to prolonged separation from our family and friends, to ridiculously frugal budgets, to living with assigned companions 24/7, to constant monitoring of our emails. We can't read newspapers, surf the internet, watch TV, go to a movie, or listen to anything other than approved music. We learn new languages and cultures, adapt to different climates.

Upon returning home, Mormons must adapt again to their native culture, which surprisingly is almost as hard as leaving it was to begin with. We adapt to short engagements, quickly followed by a household of five or six children.

As a gay Mormon, I had to adjust to total abandonment by my friends, to a life without the Church that had been the focus of my existence. Ex-Mormons face a similar traumatic adjustment to their new normal.

If a convert to Mormonism can give up coffee, tea, alcohol, and tobacco to save his soul, why can't we give up meat to save civilization?

We're perfectly capable of making whatever adaptations we must to reduce greenhouse gases and limit the extent of global suffering.

We all know someone who's been forced to change careers. I went from teaching English to experimenting on rat brains to delivering mail to processing equity loans. In today's economy, few of us will escape the enormous difficulties associated with career change. Those working in oil and coal and fracking can do it as well. And the rest of us can accept the burden of helping them accomplish it.

A native of New Orleans, I evacuated with one suitcase two days before Hurricane Katrina and never saw my apartment again. I relocated to Seattle and started my life over at the age of forty-four.

If we can disrupt our lives to cope with the devastating effects of climate change, we can make the necessary adjustments to combat that climate change.

Everyone of every religion and every culture faces extreme difficulties. It's part of mortality. What's extraordinary about humans is that we even seek out difficulties on purpose. We climb Mt. Everest. We push ourselves to the limit for a five-year career in gymnastics. We spend months or years in Antarctica studying penguins. We fly to the moon, we live aboard space stations, we choose careers deactivating bombs. We spend our lives serving others as teachers, nurses, physicians, and firefighters. As bishops, Sunday School teachers, and Relief Society presidents.

Mormons believe we've come to Earth for the purpose of being tested to our absolute limits.

We can adjust to whatever changes we must to reduce carbon emissions. The truth is, if we don't do something hard now, we'll be left with no choice but to face even more severe adjustments later.

Mormons left their homes in Europe and other parts of the world and crossed the Plains on foot to start new lives in the desert.

We can adjust to climate combat.

So let's start singing the Handcart song and get to work.

# Missing the Forest for the (Dead) Trees

"It's snowing in South Carolina," a friend told me. "So much for global warming, huh?"

We hear these sarcastic dismissals of climate change almost as often as we hear reports of record high temperatures.

Climate change deniers are missing the forest for the (dead) trees.

No climatologist ever claimed there would be record high temperatures every day in every location around the world. But twisting what scientists mean by global warming into something preposterous is the only way fossil fuel advocates can appear to have an even remotely successful rebuttal.

Straw men burn easily and do nothing but add more greenhouse gases to the atmosphere.

Recently, a black professor came to speak to city employees in my town about institutional racism perpetuated by dominant white culture. She began her lecture with, "When I say 'white culture,' I don't mean *every* white person. I mean the dominant culture as a whole."

She found it necessary to say this at the start of every discussion because inevitably when she brought up an example of institutional racism, someone in the audience would say, "But I don't do that!" As if the fact that a single person didn't commit this or that particular act of discrimination proved discrimination didn't exist at all.

The outlier defense seems to be the primary tactic used by climate change deniers. "The Hubbard glacier is growing. All this talk about glaciers melting is just bunk. Some grow and some shrink. That's just the way glaciers work."

How can global warming be real if every single glacier in the world isn't retreating? The same way the strongest typhoon on record can hit the Philippines while Georgia doesn't get hit by a hurricane at all. Roughly 90% of glaciers are shrinking worldwide. That's not a "he said, she said" statistic.

Likewise, while there are both record high temperatures and record low temperatures every year, the ratio of record lows to record highs gets smaller every year. For every one record low, there are more and more record highs.

More significantly, the average global temperature is rising steadily. When taking every single temperature recorded worldwide in a given year into account—the record highs, the record lows, and everything in between—we see that the warmest twenty years ever recorded have occurred in the last twenty-three years. The warmest four years ever recorded occurred in the last five.

"But New England is having a blizzard as we speak!"

Climate change deniers are missing the snowstorm for the snow. They're missing the drought for the lack of precipitation. They're missing the flooding for the rain.

When my husband and I sit on the porch to relax, I may say, "It's a bit chilly."

He'll reply, "I think it's cold."

I may say, "Looks like a little light rain today."

He'll reply, "No, it's just drizzling."

"Ooh, kinda hot out here," I remark.

"It's cool in the shade."

This kind of thing drives me crazy even after eleven years of marriage. I want to say, "You're missing the big picture. Stop focusing on the tiny details and understand the *point*."

Many politicians and pundits in the media keep saying, "Voters are tired of political extremes. They want leaders who will compromise."

Whether those extremes are Medicare for All, tuition-free college, or drastic action to address climate change, polls suggest that a majority actually support these policies. By definition, these positions aren't extreme.

The next time our climate change denying neighbor or coworker or uncle says, "Global warming isn't real. It snowed in Mississippi," we need to tailor a response they'll understand.

Perhaps something like this: "If you want, I can take care of your lawn the next time it needs mowing. Are you okay with me spraying Round Up on 90% of it? It's not like your lawn will be dead. 10% of it will still look fabulous."

"That's a great business report! Do you mind if we tell the boss I did 90% of the work and you did just 10%? It's not like I'm taking credit or anything. Your name will still be on the report."

Global warming is real. We can't afford to let our friends and family miss the explanation for the words.

# Fossil Fuels Anonymous

We need literal, real treatment for our addiction to fossil fuels.

When I was a teenager, my uncle told me to get a job on an oil rig in the Gulf of Mexico. An introverted reader so clean and careful with my books they still looked brand new when I'd finished them, I was appalled by the idea of being covered in sweat and oil for days at a time. But my uncle insisted we were put on Earth to suffer and that I should always reject the easy path.

I thought his philosophy was nuts. Now, though, when I think back on this incident, what I'm most grateful for is the knowledge I didn't earn a living, however temporarily, in a field so destructive to our environment. I've seen friends and family do just that, earning good money, living in nicer homes than I ever will, comfortable and proud to be successful in life, refusing to recognize their contribution to the global disaster developing around us.

Despite the many Puritan aspects of U.S. culture, for the most part we and the rest of the industrialized world worship comfort almost more than we worship money. We spend $20 on over-the-counter meds to treat our cold, and when that doesn't work, we rush to the doctor and demand antibiotics despite knowing they'll have no effect on viral infections.

But we want to feel better *now*. We take dangerously high dosages of acetaminophen, aware of the risk to our liver, to get rid of that headache *now*. And this obsessive need for comfort is just as strong when we're feeling well. We have seat warmers in our cars. We pay $3000 for a mattress. We make toilets that wash our butts. Our toilet seats have warmers, too.

Most of these things aren't bad. I'm a big fan of comfort myself. The problem is that this mindset leaves us unprepared to accept the loss of comfort inherent in adequately addressing climate breakdown.

Among the multitude of adaptations we need to make include imposing a limit on meat consumption and mandating a two-child limit on families. We need to move away from a tourism economy that encourages people to drive across the country or fly around the world every chance they get. We need to cut down on single-family cars, regulate mileage, and develop more comprehensive public transportation. We need to regulate heating and cooling in both homes and businesses. We need to divert taxes from the military to retrofit every rooftop in America with solar panels or white paint, replace every poorly made window with energy-efficient windows. We need to relocate entire communities from areas it's already too late to save. We need to ban all fracking and all new drilling, even if that means creating a new Public Works Administration to address the accompanying job loss.

Does any of this sound too "uncomfortable"? Too disruptive? These are almost certainly the easiest of the shifts we must accept if we want to slow down climate change long enough to adapt to it.

The good news is we're perfectly capable of making significant changes when we set our minds to it. A murderous husband laced his wife's Tylenol with cyanide thirty-five years ago. Now we put safety seals on every medicine and applicable food product.

A terrorist tried to blow up a plane with explosives hidden in his shoes. Now millions of people take their shoes off in airports every year.

The newly blind learn Braille. Women (and men) give up their breasts to survive cancer. People with sleep apnea adjust to uncomfortable CPAP machines to live through the night.

Elderly folks learn how to use computers and cell phones. Alcoholics and addicts learn to live without their drug of choice. We adapt. It's one of the most profound traits exhibited by the human species.

We adapt in our personal lives all the time. After earning three English degrees, I decided to take a different path and earned a Biology degree. I hate needles, passing out twice in my youth when doctors gave me injections. I always "knew" that if I ever developed diabetes, I'd kill myself rather than face a lifetime of daily injections. Now I give myself two injections a day without a second thought. Reducing my carb intake is a tougher challenge, but again, what's the alternative? We do what we have to do.

We can make hard changes. We can make scary changes. We can make difficult changes that negatively impact us physically, emotionally, and financially but which are still essential to our well-being and survival.

We need to ask ourselves if giving up hamburgers or Hummers or holidays in Paris is a greater loss of comfort than living with increasingly severe droughts, floods, hurricanes, wildfires, and crop failures.

We need to create a new twelve-step program, Fossil Fuels Anonymous. A real program, not a metaphorical one. We're addicted to fossil fuels, to the comfort and convenience they give us, and we've hit rock bottom. Instead of alcoholism leading us to lose our jobs, homes, and families, fossil fuel addiction is leading us to lose those same jobs, homes, and families, our entire ecosystem and, ultimately, civilization.

Scientists have been trying to force an intervention on us, but we keep singing Amy Winehouse's "Rehab" to drown out their voices. Recovery from fossil fuels will probably take more than twelve steps, unfortunately, and it will require a rather intensive program, but we can't afford to put it off, and we can't afford to relapse.

If we want to survive our addiction, we'd better get started right away—before we overdose on the most dangerous drug our species has ever known...and never wake up.

# Let's Put a Brake on Traffic Pollution

We've long known about air pollution and water pollution. We know about toxic waste, oil spills, and islands of plastic floating about the ocean. We even understand the negative impacts of light pollution and noise pollution. But we need to add traffic to the list of pollutants that diminish our quality of life.

It's not any particular emission that qualifies traffic as pollution. If every single car and truck on the road today no longer emitted any waste at all, the sheer number of vehicles would still be detrimental to our health.

Long, slow, daily commutes, often in stop-and-go traffic, take an emotional toll, decreasing productivity at work and increasing tension in both our professional and personal relationships. The financial burden of car payments, insurance, upkeep, gas, and parking add additional stress. Accidents, detours, and road construction bring us closer and closer to the breaking point. Almost every day, we hear about another incident of road rage, sparked by virtually anything.

I drove for twenty years and noticed my irritability on the road growing daily. One day, annoyed when the car ahead of me took too long to make a left turn, I honked. But as I drove on, I realized that the driver of the other car had become enraged, far out of proportion to the offense. His tires squealing, he made a loop and raced to catch up with me.

Driving right alongside me, he rolled down his window and cursed and shouted and gestured and honked and honked.

I realized I could have been killed over a minor, brief irritation. My honking, after all, had also been out of proportion to the insult of waiting a few extra seconds for him to turn.

But both of us were already primed to explode because of the toxic influence of traffic. Millions of drivers are kept at an emotional temperature only a few degrees short of boiling. With just a tiny bit of additional heat, that boiling point is quickly reached.

Yet even if there were no threat of violence at all, even if there weren't 40,000 deaths from automobile accidents in the U.S. each year, traffic pollution would continue to steal too much life from our day. And it does this *every* day, day after day after day. We hate when someone cuts us off. We hate when someone steals our parking space. We hate when drivers in the next lane refuse to acknowledge our blinkers and either speed up or slow down to let us move over.

We hate signs that are so confusing we miss our exit. We hate driving around and around looking for a place to park on the street. We hate when the person in front of us doesn't know where they're going. We hate huge box trucks in our lane blocking all visual input from the road ahead. We hate that each time it rains, every other driver on the road seems never to have experienced driving in the rain before.

The list could go on and on. I expect it would be impossible for most drivers to read this list without immediately coming up with several animated additions of their own.

Given our population, it's unlikely we can do anything to fully eradicate the problem of traffic pollution from modern society. That doesn't mean, however, we can't lessen its impact. And alleviating a problem is better than ignoring it.

Third Avenue in downtown Seattle where I work is a normal, main thoroughfare most of the day. But during both morning and afternoon rush hour, the street is closed to all traffic other than public transportation. Police monitor and give tickets to any drivers who feel they're exempt.

When I lived in New Orleans, Bourbon Street in the French Quarter was routinely blocked to traffic during heavy pedestrian activity. For Mardi Gras, almost the entire French Quarter was free of cars. Many other cities around the world also recognize the benefit of restricting cars from certain areas.

Large parts of Copenhagen are free of cars, a huge section of Quebec City, a substantial portion of Guadalajara. Significant areas of Havana and Bogotá are car free, a large portion of Fes el Bali in Morocco, several of the islands making up Hong Kong, and the city center in Fazilka, India. Brussels has created the second largest car-free area in Europe.

In Minneapolis, overhead pedestrian passageways connect buildings in eighty downtown blocks. Some cities also offer underground walking to connect downtown blocks. Louvain-la-Neuve in Belgium still allows cars downtown, but only on subterranean roads. Parking there is only allowed underground as well. Toronto, Edmonton, Montreal, and Calgary also provide either pedestrian tunnels or elevated walkways. There's more than one way to address the problem. But even offering pedestrians alternatives doesn't truly erase the toxic effect of traffic.

When we create these car-free zones, we can certainly make exemptions for public transportation, delivery trucks, mail carriers, waste management, and vehicles driven by people with disabilities. Carrying groceries on a bus isn't the easiest thing to do, made even more difficult if there are two or three young children in tow.

We'd still need additional cultural changes to make car-free zones work. More benches not specifically tied to public transportation, with overhead cover to protect pedestrians from rain, snow, or sun. The addition of more Mom and Pop grocery stores. Economic incentives to keep businesses in areas people will be reluctant at first to support. Regulations triggering the expansion of those car-free zones if people simply move all their traffic farther out to the suburbs in an attempt to evade them. And many other accommodations to sustain a traffic-reduced lifestyle.

Twenty years have passed since I gave up my car, and it's a decision I've never regretted. God knows the current state of public transportation hasn't brought me to Nirvana, but supporting car-free zones could help reduce toxic stress caused by too many cars and trucks as well as too few buses and trains. Let's recognize traffic congestion as more than an annoyance. It is harmful pollution we must clean up so we can live healthier, happier lives.

# Climate Change Deniers Are Committing Mass Murder-Suicide

According to Josephus, in the year 73 CE, a group of 960 Jewish rebels chose to commit mass suicide rather than be captured by the Romans. In 1997, over three dozen members of the Heaven's Gate cult committed suicide together. Almost two decades earlier, followers of Jim Jones committed mass suicide as well, more than 900 people found dead in their jungle Utopia.

We'll probably never know exactly what happened at Masada, but a handful of survivors of the Jonestown massacre revealed that adult cult members were ordered by Jones to administer cyanide to their children before drinking it themselves. Over 300 of those killed were children. While I feel suicide is a viable personal choice for people under virtually all circumstances, dragging others to the grave who don't want to go is a horrific, barbaric crime.

Climate change deniers are committing mass murder-suicide, and we must fight for our lives. Many of us are worried about hurting others in almost any kind of interaction, and so we tend to "fight" in a calm, civil manner.

I suppose there's room for that approach, but how often does asking a murderer nicely not to kill you succeed as a tactic?

Pleading with their killers didn't save Sharon Tate or her friends.

Throwing down their weapons and surrendering didn't save the 300 black Union soldiers at Fort Pillow during the American Civil War. Cooperating with their oppressors didn't end well for those European Jews who chose not to "make trouble."

Today, as we face global warming and an increasing rate of extinction among the planet's various species, pleading or surrendering or cooperating isn't going to save us. Many on the left feel that electing Democrats will solve the problem, but a sizable number of Democrats take money from the fossil fuel industry and quietly but firmly support fracking, new pipelines, and more drilling.

If a family member is the one killing you, are you any less dead?

When I see the consistent lack of action to implement common sense gun regulations after the latest mass murder by an active shooter, I wonder how we can ever hope to mobilize enough people to address the even more daunting danger of climate change.

One of my students revealed she had a glass eye because she'd been shot in the face by her ex-boyfriend. She'd broken up with the guy and eventually started dating another young man. One evening, her ex-boyfriend barged in and shot them both. As they lay bleeding on the living room floor, the student's new boyfriend whispered for her to play dead. She did, listening in terror as she heard her ex banging on her mother's bedroom door. Then she heard him shoot one more time.

The student's new boyfriend died that evening, as did the ex. Her mother climbed out her bedroom window and ran to the neighbor's house to call the police. My student crawled to her sister's bedroom and begged for help. Her sister had been lying in bed listening to music on her headphones and been completely unaware of the carnage happening just down the hall.

Almost every day, we hear about a husband who has killed his wife and then himself. We hear about a mother who has killed her children and then herself. We hear about a pilot who deliberately brings a plane down to kill others so his own death will be remembered. We hear about suicide bombers killing shoppers at a market as he blows his own body to pieces. The Columbine school shooters killed themselves after killing their classmates.

Murder-suicide is so common that we can all think of half a dozen other examples without even trying.

Some people, of course, kill without meaning to. The captain of the Titanic didn't *mean* to kill 1500 people, but he brought some of the most privileged people in the world to an early end. Likewise, while some of the people who refuse to address the devastating effects of carbon emissions do so deliberately in the hope of creating dire conditions to trigger the Second Coming of the Messiah, others think they can get away with their recklessness and don't intentionally mean to bring about so much death.

But motivation isn't particularly relevant. Politicians and CEOs and shareholders, voters and consumers, anyone who advocates for fossil fuels, is pointing a gun at our heads.

Some of us are listening to music with our headphones, completely oblivious to the danger.

Committing suicide as a species is a viable choice, I suppose, but not *all* of us want to die. Go ahead and kill yourself if you must, but don't take the rest of us with you.

In the movie *Alive*, based on the true story of the Andes plane crash survivors, there's a scene where Nando, one of the soccer players who has taken a leadership position in the days after the crash, argues with another survivor who wants to take a different route to reach help. As they argue, Nando demands that a third member of the escape team chime in on the decision. The third guy refuses to take sides. "I'll do whatever you guys decide."

This infuriates Nando, who says something to the effect of, "This is a life and death decision. One of us is right and the other is going to end up getting us all killed. Don't you *care* which decision we make?"

Too many of us are content to let others fight the battles of reducing fossil fuel emissions and developing less dangerous energy usage. But *our* lives are on the line. If we play dead, we may actually end up dead. If we manage to survive, we still risk losing our loved ones.

Entire communities commit suicide, sometimes with the most noble of goals. At the moment, our entire civilization is making that same choice, for both noble and ignoble reasons. And murdering those who won't go along willingly.

We need to fight back...while we still have a fighting chance.

# Palliative Care for Humanity

We need to stop wasting money trying to fix things that can't be fixed. We've chosen not to address climate change in a meaningful way, and that makes the fights for better jobs, universal healthcare, tuition-free college, equal rights, humane immigration policies, and almost everything else *pointless*.

Instead, it would be better to spend the last few decades of human civilization offering palliative care. Treating cataracts or repairing obstetric fistulas in Third World countries costs little and allows us to greatly, if temporarily, improve the quality of life for millions. We can redirect funds from the space program to support food banks and homeless shelters, siphon off funds from medical research to support aid in dying.

Making no further attempt to cure deadly diseases sounds heartless. But the whole point of palliative care is to accept the reality of imminent death. I watched my mother die of leukemia at the age of forty-three. I watched my husband die of liver cancer at sixty-one, a year before he planned to retire. I understand *wanting* to live and *wanting* our loved ones to survive.

But there's no sense wasting money on lost causes or giving people false hope. We could conceivably develop a cure for all diseases, and it will mean nothing within a few decades as people free of every cancer cell die from the cataclysmic effects of unchecked climate change.

Lots of perfectly healthy people died when the Titanic went down.

Over 14,000 homes were destroyed in last fall's California wildfires. When Hurricane Katrina struck, I evacuated my hometown of New Orleans with one suitcase and never looked back. I instinctively knew the city's fate was sealed, that there was no point rebuilding. I moved to Seattle and started my life over at the age of forty-four. It sucks, no question about it, but those of us who live in the areas most vulnerable to the effects of climate change will *have* to move sooner or later. In fact, relocating vulnerable communities is the *least* drastic of the measures we need to begin taking immediately.

I've spent most of my writing career focused on the inequalities and abuses of the Mormon Church, hoping to help the Church move toward more humane policies. If there's been any advance, though, it's so minimal I can't afford to invest any more time and energy in that project. It's a lost cause.

Many if not most of us have dedicated a huge portion of our lives to lost causes. It's time to focus on the bare essentials—stopping the progression of climate change and surviving what's already on the way.

A future without a complete mobilization to address climate change is one with increasingly extreme floods, droughts, fires, massive crop failures, water shortages, and wars over resources.

Successful mobilization entails an immediate end to all new fossil fuel extraction, processing, storage, and pipelines. All fossil fuel subsidies redirected toward solar, wind, wave, and other renewables or "green" energy. The redirection of hundreds of billions of dollars from the military to renewables as well and the infrastructure to support them.

That's just the beginning, I'm afraid. It will take a lot more than this. But we don't *have* to fight to survive. It unfortunately appears we've already made that decision. We can most certainly choose palliative care instead.

If a world of increasing misery and destruction is what we want, we can continue to put all our money and effort into our favorite lost causes. Perhaps making ourselves feel good about our personal moral compass is a form of palliative care as well.

If a civilization torn apart by unchecked climate change is *not* what we want, then we need to invest everything into a full-scale battle against fossil fuels, now.

# Dead Mankind Walking

Have you ever waited in a crowded emergency room, sick, in pain, miserable, and watched for hours as patients who came in long after you arrived were treated first? It's frustrating, no matter how much sympathy we have for others.

But that's not the situation we're confronted with now. It's no longer a matter of waiting a few extra hours before every problem in the room is addressed. Instead, we're on a bloody battlefield where Army doctors must decide in seconds who will be left to die so they can save others who still have a fighting chance to survive their wounds. Every person on planet Earth now faces the triage of climate breakdown.

Recent reports show that the global calamity in our very near future is even worse than we thought, and we already knew it was going to be bad. No matter *what* we do, many of the harshest consequences can no longer be avoided, and those that can will require more sacrifice and suffering than we've ever endured. In the face of a task so overwhelming, with such little hope for success, it's easier to let the next generation deal with it, easier to throw up our hands and say it can't be done, easier to say, "Let's eat, drink, and be merry, for tomorrow we die."

But we *can* do this. We just need a Manhattan Project—a Pangaea Project, if you will—that we invest in as if winning the war depended on it.

I saw Marlo Thomas in a fundraising film supporting St. Jude Hospital, talking with the mother of a young child who was saved through radical and extensive treatment. "It's a miracle," the woman said in relieved gratitude.

In a pleasant but firm voice, Marlo Thomas corrected her. "No," she said. "It's science."

Human beings can accomplish extremely ambitious and incredible things, build pyramids, lay transatlantic cable, manipulate DNA, construct space stations, and study stars a hundred thousand light years away. We simply need to realize—*today*—that it's up to us to save ourselves from the increasingly dire effects of climate change.

I was born and raised in New Orleans, with its wonderful if flawed culture. The motto of The City That Care Forgot was "Laissez les bons temps rouler." I spent years enjoying Mardi Gras in the French Quarter, riding the streetcar along St. Charles Avenue past the city's most prestigious homes, listening to live music on Jackson Square.

But when Hurricane Katrina struck, I knew instinctively there was no point going back. Under the best of circumstances, the city was still below sea level, with more of the surrounding marshland disappearing every day. It was inevitable that another, even more cataclysmic hurricane was going to impact this vulnerable city again.

I evacuated with one suitcase and never saw my apartment again, relocating to the Pacific Northwest. I was not going to spend the rest of my life rebuilding a doomed city. I cut my losses and ran, unwilling to succumb to the "sunk cost" fallacy that seemed to guide so many others.

As a child, I subscribed to *Ranger Rick*. I watched the Australian TV show *Barrier Reef*. As an adult, I donated to The Nature Conservancy, the World Wildlife Fund, The American Chestnut Foundation, Earthjustice, American Forests, the Natural Resources Defense Council, the League of Conservation Voters, Rainforest Action Network, and other conservation groups. In a perfect world, I would continue giving to *every* conservation group.

But several years ago, because of its political and physical environment, I stopped donating to plant trees in Israel. This seemed a battle we could no longer win. When the Sierra Club in Seattle organized their efforts into pulling up invasive blackberry bushes—a nuisance I couldn't even manage in my own yard—I determined their goals were unrealistic.

So I redirected my limited funds to other organizations like Greenpeace, applauding as their activists physically blocked an oil company's icebreaker from leaving Portland, preventing it from heading to the Arctic to assist in drilling. 350.org, which also demands drastic measures to address climate crisis, is on my list as well, as is solutionsearch.org.

As a teenager, I read a great deal of Holocaust literature. I determined to hire my father, a contractor, to build a secret room in the home he would one day construct for me, so I could hide Jews if the need ever arose again. As a Mormon, my family stored a year's supply of food to prepare us for the tribulations of the Last Days, a tradition I continued long after I became an atheist. I also kept a valid passport at all times in case I had to flee the country at a moment's notice. I thought of various ways to ensure I had a fighting chance to survive whatever horrible disaster, man-made or natural, might occur.

Then one day, in my mid-fifties, living with both HIV and diabetes, I had an epiphany. I wasn't going to be one of the survivors. Rather than feeling devastated, I found the realization liberating. Instead of worrying about myself, I could focus on what was best to help others.

I don't mean to sound overly altruistic. It was pure practicality on my part.

In the film *The Day After Tomorrow*, when the world is faced with an abrupt new ice age, a NOAA paleoclimatologist makes an astonishing demand of the Vice President of the United States. The scientist draws a horizontal line across the center of a map of the U.S. and says, "Evacuate everyone south of that line."

The Vice President can't believe what he's hearing. "What about the people in the north?"

The scientist pauses for a moment and then blurts out the awful truth. "I'm afraid it's too late for them."

The Vice President questions both the climatologist's assessment and his motive until learning from the man's superior that the scientist's own son is stranded in New York, well north of that triage line.

It's worth noting, I suppose, that our planet will survive climate change. Life itself will survive. That's happened after every other mass extinction event, too. Most of us are aware we're already well into the first mass extinction event caused not by meteorites or supervolcanoes but by human activity, and that this process is escalating, not ameliorating.

Still, it seems more likely than not that at least some of the billions of humans on the planet will survive. But the question remains whether human civilization will also survive the global upheaval taking place before our very eyes.

In the U.S., we're used to seeing disasters on a limited scale. Katrina killed between two to three thousand. Tornadoes and wildfires may kill a few dozen. We forget that even in relatively recent history, those numbers aren't at all representative of what humans as a species face under "normal" fluctuations in the environment, much less the numbers we'll rack up from the unprecedented environmental conditions in our near future.

A half million people were killed by a 1970 cyclone in Bangladesh, the kind of storm climatologists predict will become more and more common as the oceans continue to warm. Up to 2,000,000 were killed in the 1887 Yellow River flood in China. An astonishing 4,000,000 died in the flooding which struck China in 1931. And we're expecting more and more extreme flood events as the Earth's temperatures rise.

Of course, those rising temperatures alone can kill. 55,000 people died from the 2010 heat wave in Russia. 70,000 died across Europe from the heat wave in 2003. Global warming will only make deadly heat waves like these more common in the coming years.

Then there are famines. In the late 1840's, a million and a half people starved to death in Ireland. A French famine from 1693 to 1694 killed two million. A famine in India between 1896 and 1902 killed six million, a number so high we instantly associate it with the Holocaust.

Somewhere between 15,000,000 and 43,000,000 Chinese starved to death between 1958 and 1961. The Holocaust times seven. We've all read at least one analysis pointing out that one of the consequences of climate change will be widespread crop failure.

This brief list of massive death tolls doesn't even begin to address mortality from disease. Between fifty million and one hundred million people died in the 1918 Spanish flu pandemic, the disease spreading to virtually every inhabited spot on the planet. The bubonic plague killed off between one and two thirds of the entire population of Europe in the space of a few years. *The Coming Plague: Newly Emerging Diseases in a World Out of Balance*, by Laurie Garrett, gives us a glimpse of what we can expect in the next few decades, and it isn't pretty.

These aren't exhaustive lists. And it's exactly this level of widespread mortality we're looking at in the face of unchecked climate change. We'd better get used to hearing those numbers routinely again. It might be sobering to remember that most of those vast numbers were racked up in times when the global population was billions and billions lower than it is now. Future death tolls, if there will be any encyclopedia to record them, will undoubtedly be far larger, since the precipitating events will be much larger themselves.

There will be many lives, both human and not, which we won't be able to save.

We all have our favorite species—the gray wolf, the spotted owl, the orca—but we need to keep our focus. When I received an email the other day from a conservation group begging for donations to save the marbled murrelet, I had that epiphany once again. This species is not going to make it. Its fate has already been decided.

In May of 2018, California's economy was ranked as the fifth largest in the entire world, even beating out the UK. By early November of 2018, the state had recorded its worst fire season ever, with fifteen of the twenty worst fire seasons in the state's history occurring since the year 2000. After years of drought, every single part of the state was under either high or extreme threat of wildfire. While flames were destroying celebrity homes in Malibu, the city of Paradise in northern California was almost completely obliterated.

What would happen if the U.S. lost the agricultural bounty of California? What kind of repercussions would the loss of the world's fifth largest economy have on the rest of the world's finances? And what can we expect globally given that climate change clearly affects more than just this one vital area?

I think most of us already know we need to take action. Like the obese man who knows he needs to change his eating habits but can't quite make himself do it, we're faced not only with climate change but also with our own hesitation. That hesitation exists on an individual level but also on an organizational level, on a political level, on a religious level.

But we no longer have the luxury of patience. So what do we do?

Malcolm Gladwell's *The Tipping Point: How Little Things Can Make a Big Difference*, explains that we don't need to force an entire culture to change to make a big impact. The book's blurb reads, "The tipping point is that magic moment when an idea, trend, or social behavior crosses a threshold, tips, and spreads like wildfire." Gladwell clarifies the sociology behind and the traits necessary to spread social change.

We are a narcissistic society. We're taught to seek immediate gratification. Corporate culture has arguably always been unhealthy for society, but now a CEO may only be at the head of any given business for a year or two. He or she is after quick profits, even at the expense of long-term success for the corporation. Employees no longer work at the same company for twenty or thirty years. Most of us bounce around from workplace to workplace. We don't even have roots in our communities anymore because we move all over the country. Everything is temporary.

Recently, I went to buy a new printer for my home computer. The salesperson suggested I buy the cheapest one and then toss it when the ink ran out because it would be cheaper to buy an entirely new printer than replace the ink cartridges. Do I even need to bother explaining the repercussions this pervasive attitude in our culture has on the environment?

While we're already experiencing devastating effects from climate change at this very moment, many of the worst are another ten or twenty years away. How do we get anyone, including ourselves, to act *now* and not put it off till we're more stable financially, till the kids are grown, till we're retired and have more time?

"You are not obligated to complete the work [of perfecting the world]," the Pirkei Avot tells us, "but neither are you free to desist from it."

My husband has a flexible schedule. His strength is to go to rallies and protests and government meetings. He'll do all of that, much of which is both boring and exhausting, but he won't wear a sweater or jacket in the house so we can use less fuel for heating, which to me seems like a simple matter.

The thing is, we *all* have quirks and imperfections. Rather than beat ourselves for our weaknesses or criticize others for theirs, we have to accept human nature for what it is and focus on what we are individually willing to do. We don't need to make this about guilt for ourselves or anyone else. Guilt is a horribly inefficient motivator. We need real motivation.

At the same time, we can't wait around for someone else to say just the right thing to convince us. We must personally make the final persuasive arguments that fit our own personalities. It's no one else's duty to inspire us to commit. That's our job. When I was first diagnosed with HIV, I was angry at the man who'd infected me for not even telling me he was positive. Then I realized it wasn't up to him to protect me. My health was *my* responsibility, and I'd blown it.

Blaming others for our inaction may make it easier to look in the mirror, but it won't protect us from the real, physical consequences of rationalizing this as someone else's fault.

Unfortunately, even humans with the best of intentions will have disagreements on which actions to take, but we need to redirect as much energy away from infighting toward corrective action instead.

Some people may be able to return to school and train to work in a field that allows them to spend forty or more hours a week addressing climate change directly. Others can speak up in their church or synagogue or mosque or coven and try to influence their faith community. Some can pen op-eds to influence public opinion, perhaps rally people to understand that in the battle between government interference and personal liberty, we've entered a period when climatic martial law is needed.

A person can store a year's supply of food during normal times, but during war, it becomes a crime to hoard. The emergency we face requires us to act differently than we do in peacetime. The point is to do what *we* are capable of doing, and to support those who can do what we can't.

Michael Callen, author of *Surviving AIDS*, was an early AIDS activist. Diagnosed with full-blown AIDS for over ten years, Callen's goal was to hang on long enough for the development of better treatment.

He died shortly before the new life-saving drug cocktails came out. At this point in ecological history, we need to do what we can to get by until we find a way to deal effectively with greenhouse gases. Civilization may collapse before we achieve that, but we have no choice other than to try.

And yet we *do* have a choice, don't we? We can choose to commit suicide. It's not only individuals who can make such decisions, an entire species can collectively do it as well. We've watched as a formation of fighter jets at an air show fly in perfect synchronization—right into the ground, not deliberate suicide, but simply the result of following a mistaken leader. I certainly hope that, both individually and collectively, we can accept that doing the Grim Reaper's job for him isn't the best way to deal with our current predicament.

With every new report on the escalation of global warming, I remember the classic episode of *Star Trek: The Next Generation* titled "The Inner Light." Captain Picard, under the control of an alien object, experiences the final days of a doomed civilization as a member of that race. Scientists on the planet, devoid of life now for millennia, had realized their sun was growing warmer and that all life on their planet would soon cease.

They weren't advanced enough to build ships to transport survivors to another world, so they created a device that would let members of other sentient species live an entire lifetime on their planet by proxy while unconscious. They hoped that in this way at least someone would know who they were and remember them fondly.

Will our Voyager probe be the only thing left of our vast civilization for inhabitants of other star systems to know about us?

We need to remember we're in a triage situation. We're keeping our ninety-seven-year-old grandmother with Alzheimer's on life support when we don't have the resources to do so. No matter how wonderful a person our grandmother is, no matter how much we love her and want her to stay, we can't defy the biological reality of death. We need to invest our time, money, energy, and intellectual ability elsewhere.

Is that creating a "death panel"? Are we playing God? While some of these human examples are metaphors, probably not all of them are. In a triage situation, if you choose to save one person, you're often simultaneously choosing not to save another.

You *cannot* save everyone. We can try to save the murrelet or we can fight fossil fuels. We can try to eradicate blackberry bushes or we can work to curtail meat consumption. If we find that accepting the principle of climatic triage violates our ethics, and we therefore insist on pouring everything into saving the unsavable, the most likely outcome is we'll lose everything. That's not a hypothetical situation. It's the very definition and purpose of triage.

We can't waste any more time on lost causes, even the worthiest of lost causes. It is time for drastic, strategic, life-altering action.

We must devote our resources to dealing with climate change. We must fight to ban *all* fracking, *all* new pipelines, *all* new drilling. We must invest heavily, drastically, strategically in every form of "greener" energy possible, solar, wind, wave, and any other type we can think of. Every tax break and subsidy going to fossil fuel corporations must be redirected to developing renewables. We must divert billions, even hundreds of billions, from the defense budget toward addressing climate change, a more powerful and existential threat than Russia or China ever were.

Of *course* we don't want to do this. It's scary. It's expensive. It's inconvenient. We'll lose power, or control, or social standing. We feel nervous about what might be required of us. Making the necessary drastic changes will disrupt our lives significantly in ways we don't like.

We have a *Sophie's Choice* between temporary comfort and long-term survival.

We must remember the story of Aron Ralston, who was trapped in a desert canyon, his right forearm pinned under a boulder. He tried for six days to free himself, to wait for rescue, to hope everything could end well. But he finally came to a horrifying conclusion. If he didn't take drastic measures, he was going to die.

At that point, there was no more consideration of how to save his arm. His arm, he realized, was already lost. The question now was whether he could save the rest of himself, save his very life. So he made the gut-wrenching decision to pull out his dull pocketknife and get to work.

*This* is where we're at, folks. There's no returning to a normal life. Normal life is over. That choice has already been made. If we don't want to die, we must accept the facts as they are.

It's time to cut off our arm.

# Grab What We Can and Run

Addressing the climate emergency means losing much of the life and culture we love.

On Friday, August 26, 2005, I went to a local performance of *Hair* in Uptown New Orleans. The cast did a fine job, and I had a pleasant evening with a good friend.

The next morning, Paul called me. "Are you evacuating?"

"Huh?"

"There's a major hurricane in the Gulf. I'm going to my sister's house in Baton Rouge. Are you going to stay with your family?"

The last time I'd evacuated, my partner Tom and I had been trapped on a congested highway for many hours, inching painfully along in sweltering heat. We watched as someone from the car ahead of us jumped out, ran to a nearby Dairy Queen, and came back with food for her family before the car had moved ahead twenty feet.

Another driver hopped out of his car and urinated on the side of the road in full view of dozens of families, with few other options open to him.

"I don't know," I said. "I'm so tired." Tom had died three months earlier of liver cancer. I'd spent the time since distributing his belongings, straightening out his affairs, and moving into an apartment, all while not losing any hours at work, since I'd used up my leave during Tom's illness. I'd made sure my new place had washer/dryer hookups before signing the lease, but only after I moved in did I realize the laundry doorway was smaller than normal. The appliances Tom and I had didn't fit, and smaller ones were outrageously expensive. But the new machines were in, I was settling down, and I just wanted a weekend to relax.

"Johnny," he said, "it's a category 5."

I turned on the news. While threatening storms often veered away at the last minute, I decided I'd better leave, just to be safe. I grabbed a suitcase, threw in a week's worth of meds, my journal, and a couple of changes of clothes. Before I zipped the lid shut, I evaluated the situation once more. Then I shrugged and threw in my passport, my birth certificate, and my resumé. I grabbed Tom's ashes. Then I climbed into my car and drove off.

Several hours later, I arrived at my aunt's home in Hammond, sixty miles away.

I never saw my apartment again.

When the electricity finally came back on at my aunt's placee, I jumped on the computer and bought a plane ticket to Seattle. Tom had loved our visits to the city, and since I had to go somewhere, I figured it might as well be there. I didn't choose the earliest possible flight, however. I picked September 11, 2005, hoping to create a positive association with that date.

Searching for a job and an apartment in mid-life in an unfamiliar city wasn't easy. Despite the friends I've made here in the Pacific Northwest, and finding a wonderful, loving husband, I lost something when Katrina hit. I lost my past. I lost most of my circle of friends. I lost a world I knew and loved.

*But not evacuating wouldn't have changed that.* The hurricane was on a collision course. Even though it weakened before making landfall, the destruction was unavoidable by that point. My choice wasn't whether to keep the life I had or to evacuate. The choice was to evacuate or become another of the hurricane's many victims.

Choosing not to address the climate crisis won't stop the devastation heading our way. Building new pipelines and storage facilities and drilling new wells won't weaken the storm bearing down on us. If anything, such decisions will only ensure it remains a category 5 until landfall.

Perhaps we'll even be forced to create a category 6 classification.

While poor neighborhoods in New Orleans were impacted the most, the devastation reached every level of society. Fats Domino's house, which my father had helped build, was badly damaged. Two attorneys I know owned three homes together. One received five feet of water. Another received eight feet. My friends couldn't be sure how deep the water got at the third location because nothing at all was left of the house by which to gauge.

But water didn't even need to be especially deep to destroy. One library branch where I worked only received six inches of water, but that water remained in the building for a full week in 95-degree weather. By the time anyone was able to get back inside, every book in the building was covered in mold.

The collapse of infrastructure is every bit as destructive as a storm surge.

The grocery store that served my New Orleans neighborhood only opened again in 2019, fourteen years after it was destroyed. The last branch of the public library to reopen did so that same year. Yes, there will be survivors of climate crisis even if we do nothing, but they won't have a functioning infrastructure for a very long time. Much longer than fourteen years.

Addressing climate crisis head-on won't be easy. We'll be snarled in traffic jams so stressful we'll want to turn back. And we'll only be able bring part of our lives with us. We're going to lose much that is important to us, much that we love.

Every fish in the New Orleans Aquarium died because there was no electricity to keep the water oxygenated.

Police officers blocked black pedestrians from crossing the Mississippi River Bridge from New Orleans to Gretna where there was no flooding.

Five other officers were sentenced to decades in prison for shooting a group of black people crossing a bridge over the Industrial Canal. One woman had her arm shot off by an officer's assault rifle. Two people in the group were killed and four seriously injured.

The mini-series *Five Days at Memorial*, based on a true story set in the hospital where I was born and where years later I taught nursing students, recounts the horrors of the aftermath of the storm, where forty-five patients died, some after being injected with morphine and other drugs in what many considered acts of euthanasia.

A friend of mine took part in the "looting" of a local grocery store that had lost part of its roof. With no food at home and no imminent rescue, he and others in the neighborhood waded through knee-deep, black water to get what they needed to survive.

Two of my friends refused to evacuate for Katrina because they couldn't bring their five pets with them. Luana and Margie were eventually rescued from their second-floor balcony by helicopter. They had to leave four of their pets behind.

One of my coworkers at the library lost her home and committed suicide a few months after the hurricane.

Another coworker, with an infant and a toddler, ended up at the convention center with thousands of other refugees, where they waited in sweltering heat for days, with no bathroom facilities, no food, and dead bodies decomposing throughout the crowd.

One young man who evacuated returned home, upset he still hadn't been able to contact his mother. She'd refused to evacuate with him, but rescuers had marked the house as empty of bodies, so she must have gotten out somehow.

Nope. When the young man entered to look through his ruined belongings, he found the body of his mother along with them.

An off-duty police officer called 911 from his attic, apologizing for taking the staff's time during a crisis, but explaining he was trapped in his attic and the water was still rising.

The book *1 Dead in Attic* recounts many such stories.

I mention Hurricane Katrina often when I speak of climate breakdown because it was a life-altering experience for me. For many others, it was a life-ending experience.

Not "evacuating" won't keep the devastation of climate change away. The only survivable option is to grab what we can, try to save as much of our civilization and ecosystem as we're able, and flee for our lives in stop-and-go traffic.

Lots of people burned to death in their cars trying to escape the climate-driven wildfires in Paradise last year. But not evacuating wouldn't have saved their lives. At least some of those who fled made it out.

A climate emergency is here. Ignoring it won't make it go away. We must take drastic action to save what we can. Our lives will not be the same any longer. We either accept that. Or we die.

# Chicken Little: One if by Land, Two if by Sea

When an acorn fell on Chicken Little's head, she began running around warning her fellow chickens. "The sky is falling! The sky is falling!"

For years, climate activists have been doing the same thing, running about frantically, trying to save their friends from the danger fast approaching. But politicians, and the voters who put them in office, think no more of us than they do of Chicken Little.

Now when I read another account of present (not future) climate disaster, I regret to admit I'm a little bit happy. If warnings aren't enough, perhaps consequences will be.

A native of New Orleans, I grew up knowing that flooding was "normal." One evening around 9:30, when I heard a particularly heavy downpour, I told my partner, "That's a flooding rain." I looked outside to see if the streets were clear. They were. My car was safe.

When the 10:00 news came on, the first story was, "Major flooding throughout the city." I ran back to the door and looked outside again. It was already too late. Water was halfway up the car door. Within moments, it was coming into the house. Fourteen inches of rain fell in just two hours.

Back then, when I told other people from different parts of the country about that evening, which grew much worse, they didn't believe me.

Today, twenty-five years later, people believe me without protest. Events of extreme precipitation happen often in many other places these days.

Along with more frequent flooding, we have more frequent droughts and wildfires. While it was heartbreaking to see Paradise, California obliterated, part of me felt relieved. Maybe now people would understand what we're up against if we don't take drastic action.

But no, we still don't get it. We can't pass a Green New Deal in Congress. In Washington state, where the governor's bid for the presidency is based on action to address climate change, we can't even ban fracking or new pipelines.

When the American Midwest experienced catastrophic flooding in the spring of 2019, I was…happy.

It's an awful thing to say, isn't it? I remember some of my relatives being happy when I contracted HIV. Maybe now I would repent and stop being gay. Their happiness on my behalf didn't feel as loving as they seemed to believe it was.

Even if these horrific climate disasters did finally bring about societal change, it's no longer to feel even remotely happy about them.

The past two summers in Seattle, smoke from wildfires hundreds of miles away made our air so thick with particulate matter we could often see no farther than two blocks. The news reported almost every day that our air quality was Very Unhealthy. Other days, it was Hazardous.

Almost 20% of coral reefs around the world have died in the past few decades. 15% more will likely die within the next fifteen years. Another 20% will follow in the twenty years after that. Within thirty-five more years, we'll have lost 75% of coral reefs around the world.

Indonesia has committed to moving its capital from Jakarta to a city deeper inland. In the next thirty or so years, 95% of Jakarta will be under water.

Thirty years sounds like a number too large and unreliable to worry about. But it's not the distant future. Fourteen years have already passed since Hurricane Katrina forced me to relocate thousands of miles from my hometown, and I still feel like a newcomer in Seattle.

An addict often won't seek treatment until he or she hits rock bottom. Apparently, we need to sink even deeper into the gutter of climate disaster. I keep hoping the next algae bloom or wildfire or flood or hurricane will finally open our hearts to an intervention before even more people are forced to suffer from our inaction.

What's most mystifying to me is why conservatives complain that combating climate change will cost too much.

Yes, tackling carbon emissions is expensive, but that just means *someone is going to make money*. Conservatives, don't you want it to be you?

*Someone* is going to make money developing and selling solar energy technology and products. *Someone* is going to make money developing and selling wind power technology and products. The same for wave energy and thermal energy and carbon capture.

Doesn't the Party of business want to get in on this? Promote commerce? Make millions from advances through Research and Development? In retrofitting homes and businesses?

These changes will *have* to be made sooner or later. Why not be the ones to corner the market now? The sooner we develop the products and technology, the sooner we'll make money.

Of course, we'll not only *make* money, but we'll also help limit future *losses*. Burned and flooded homes, the relocation of residents and businesses, and the widespread loss of crops all cost billions. Those losses will only increase if we don't act quickly and drastically.

Fiscal conservatives should be on board solely out of self-interest.

But they're addicted to the drugs they're on now, fossil fuels and the money derived from them.

Being Chicken Little, or even Paul Revere warning of danger by land or by sea, doesn't seem to be enough.

Sometimes, when a couple realize they need to divorce, they put it off because of the hassle in finding lawyers, dividing the assets, the cost of finding a new place to live. It's all too emotionally and financially overwhelming.

But delaying the inevitable because it's hard only prolongs the misery. We can't start building the new life we need till we finally face reality and do the hard work that must be done.

I see on the news tonight that lawmakers are still refusing to address climate change. But there's hope. Tomorrow when I turn on the TV, maybe I'll see a report about another catastrophic flood. Hurricane season starts soon, too. And wildfire season is just around the corner.

I'll keep my fingers crossed and hope the people I love won't die before they get into recovery.

*Johnny Townsend*

# What Have You Got Against a Stable Climate?

Many of the conservatives in my life aren't worried about the climate crisis because the news they watch and the people they respect tell them all is well. My sister, my niece and nephews, my aunt and cousins, my former Mormon bishop, and my other friends from church all hear the same propaganda. "The Earth has been much hotter during its lifetime. A little warming is no big deal."

What, I respond when I hear such things, have you got against a stable climate?

It's true enough that at times the Earth's climate has been warmer than it is today. We can concede that for the first 700 million years of its existence, our planet's surface was mostly molten lava. No big deal, right?

4.5 billion years is a long time, and the planet's surface has experienced widely varying temperatures during its history. Manhattan under a mile of ice is no big deal, either, I suppose.

No climate activists are denying that there have been shifts in global temperatures in the Earth's past. Most dinosaurs, except the branch that became birds, died when temperatures plummeted after a meteorite impact. That was the planet's fifth mass extinction. Of course, temperature

82

change isn't the only factor driving the current mass extinction event, but virtually all the other factors are man-made as well.

After Mt. Tambora erupted in 1815, the following year was labeled "the year without summer." Crops failed across Europe. Famines and riots claimed 200,000 lives.

That was a one-year period of climate disruption.

I've heard conservatives complain that people pushing action on climate change are only doing it because it's "good business and gives scientists jobs."

What have they got against good business and jobs?

Granted, many of us don't like the economic and physical destruction caused by some corporations, and we don't like jobs that hurt people or endanger other species. But what damage is being done by the business and jobs of climate activists? A coal miner loses the opportunity to develop black lung disease?

Coal mining is quickly going extinct regardless of climate change. People no longer earn a living from opening elevator doors, either. Jobs are lost to cultural changes, automation, and outsourcing all the time. We certainly do need stronger programs to train people for career change, but complaining that solar energy employees and scientists are stealing our jobs is not an effective strategy for accomplishing that.

I have to wonder why those who refuse to act on climate change are so against the Earth having a stable climate or at least as stable a climate as we can manage. What does that gain them?

I keep remembering Lex Luthor's plan in the first *Superman* movie. He wanted to set off nuclear bombs that would cause everything west of the San Andreas fault to sink into the ocean. Luthor bought up thousands of acres of land just to the east so he'd have prime real estate after his man-made adjustment to the coastline.

I can't help but wonder who might be buying up properties inland from Miami, Ft. Lauderdale, St. Petersburg, Daytona Beach, Tallahassee, and all the other coastal cities in Florida that will disappear over the next few decades.

We can debate approaches for addressing the climate crisis, but dismissing the need for a stable climate altogether is like saying we don't need a stable stock market, that we don't need stoplights or laws against stealing and killing. Chaos and destruction are *not* good for business or jobs. They're not good for orangutans or polar bears or palm trees. They're not good for coastal cities around the world and the hundreds of millions of people who live in them.

And they're not good, I'm afraid, even for the conservatives we love who naïvely say climate change is no big deal.

# Retrofitting Notre Dame

When a friend of mine posted a picture on Facebook of the new roof proposed for Notre Dame in Paris, I saw comments like, "It's ghastly!" and "Is this satire?" There was a "what is the world coming to?" feel to the responses, but only in the sense of good taste. No one seemed to recognize that a roof full of solar panels and a garden to raise food for the poor was exactly the kind of repairs we should be making when important structures are damaged.

In fact, we should also mandate that all existing homes and businesses be retrofitted with features to combat global warming, and that all new construction require it from the start.

When my husband and I bought a 1906 Craftsman cottage in south Seattle, we knew it would require upgrades, renovation, and repairs. That's what people *expect* when dealing with old homes. The first order of business was to replace the front door. For a hundred years, that door consisted of fifteen panes of glass.

It offered no privacy, no protection against the heat or cold, and, we soon discovered, no protection against burglary. We now have a front door made of thick pine planks. It doesn't completely fit the style of the home, but we had to make this practical adjustment. That's what living in today's world demands.

The next project on our Craftsman cottage, far larger, was to install insulation in the walls and ceiling. No one would even consider building a new home today without this basic feature. We removed the coal-burning furnace. We retrofitted our home to make it more earthquake-resistant by anchoring the walls to the foundation. We replaced eight single-pane windows with energy-efficient ones.

The bathroom in our lovely home isn't the best, but it's better than the one original to the property—an outhouse in the back yard. Just as no one today would consider purchasing an existing house or constructing a new one without a functioning bathroom, we must adjust our expectations of what's essential. Would we build a new home in the suburbs of Atlanta without installing air conditioning? Central air and heating may not be cheap, but we accept that it's a necessary expense.

Upgrading all homes and businesses to address the climate crisis is just as necessary.

But that proposal for a new roof on Notre Dame with its spire of solar panels? Is that really where we need to go?

I don't think I'll ever like the Pompidou Centre in Paris, a monstrosity of modern design surrounded by all the beautiful and traditional architecture of the 4th arrondissement. I will never like the glass pyramid in front of the Louvre blocking my view of the museum. But changes in style can't be avoided as our cultures evolve over time, regardless of climate concerns. And when those changes do involve the realities of global warming, we'll just have to live with them.

During the 1980's, the world faced a danger it had never encountered before. Bathhouses started distributing condoms to slow the spread of HIV, but many men didn't want to use them. The porn industry rose to the challenge and required adult films to show men wearing condoms to make them sexier. Porn stories in magazines were required to describe characters engaging in safer sex. The entire industry worked to change the cultural norms that were killing people.

Most guys still don't *like* condoms. They use them because survival requires it.

I don't like injecting myself with insulin twice a day. I do it because I want to reach my next birthday.

Few people enjoy colonoscopies, but we don't submit to them for fun. We do it to avoid early, preventable death.

Not every human on the planet is going to die as global temperatures continue to rise. We won't go extinct. But is losing "only" a few hundred million people, or a few billion, with the survivors suffering the cataclysms of inundated cities, crop losses and famine, and the resulting wars over resources, really the *best* way to save money? And is saving money really the *best* goal we can have?

Wouldn't it be better to replace outhouses with indoor plumbing, thin walls with insulation, and inefficient windows with efficient ones?

Notre Dame won't look the same with a solar panel roof. But after the fire, looking the same *was no longer an option* in any event. Just as status quo construction codes are no longer an option. Retrofitting existing structures and demanding more of new construction are not luxuries. They're essential.

The sooner we adapt to the reality of our new circumstances, the better off we, the buildings we love, and the planet we all live on, will be.

# Is Recycling Dinosaurs Cost Effective?

The other day, a decal on the side of a car next to the gas cap caught my eye. It displayed the traditional symbol for recycling, arrows shaped into a triangle, with the accompanying slogan: Fueled by recycled dinosaurs.

Rape jokes aren't funny. I'd like to say that jokes about raping the environment aren't funny, either, but I admit I laughed. I couldn't help but imagine Elton John repurposing one of his classics into a new hit, "The Triangle of Recycling," for a new Broadway musical, "The Exxon King."

The corporate and political will to aggressively address the climate crisis doesn't exist yet because so many policy influencers profit off the continued destruction of our climate. At what point will fossil fuels stop being cost effective, when corporate profits are offset by billions in crop losses, wildfires, floods, and other disasters? When will our lawmakers finally be forced to stop giving unprecedented tax breaks to the companies causing widespread devastation that taxpayers end up having to pay for as well?

At what point will investment in the capture, storage, and delivery of wind, wave, solar, and thermal energy become cost effective instead?

Have you ever watched the weather forecast before heading off to work? Ever evacuated for a hurricane? Prepared for a blizzard? Reacted to a tornado warning?

Each weather satellite, and there are hundreds, costs between 50 and 400 million dollars, and that doesn't include the 60 million dollars that companies like Space X charge to launch it into orbit. Hundreds of radar systems across the country cost millions more, and meteorologists, as dedicated to the public good as they may be, aren't volunteering their time.

Is that multi-million-dollar investment cost effective? Homes and businesses are still burned by wildfires and inundated by floods. So what's the point of seeing it coming?

Maybe to give us time to pile up sandbags? Open a spillway? Grab our most precious belongings and run for our lives?

Climate crisis deniers dismiss extreme meteorological events as weather, not climate change. But since the only way to measure climate change is through weather, their position is disingenuous.

If fewer people use oil, gas, and coal, shifting instead to wind, solar, and thermal, then oil companies, among the wealthiest corporations on the planet, are perfectly capable of being the ones to develop those renewable energies and the infrastructure to support them. They don't need to lose *any* portion of the market.

But even if they did, aren't conservatives always professing belief in competition and a free market?

When I was growing up, whenever my uncle was driving along a two-way country road and someone tried to pass him, he would speed up so the other driver couldn't pull into the lane ahead of him. When the other driver realized what was happening and tried to slow down and return to the lane behind my uncle, he'd slow down to prevent that as well.

He laughed when he saw a car coming down the road toward the trapped driver in the other lane.

My uncle wouldn't have lost anything if the other driver had passed him or if the other driver had fallen back behind again. Nor did he gain anything by being a prick. He just *liked* being a prick.

While transitioning from fossil fuels to renewables is not a zero-sum game, where each winner is counterbalanced by a corresponding loser, refusing to make that move is indeed a positive subtraction game where everybody loses.

What reliable business leaders give pep talks to their employees about the glories of lose/lose scenarios?

Iconic American companies like Sears and Woolworth and Kodak and Blockbuster reigned over U.S. commerce for decades. But lack of vision and adaptation to new ideas and innovations has led them each to decline or even go extinct.

There's a reason we call out of touch leaders dinosaurs.

Politicians, voters, and business leaders need to realize that the only win/win approach to combating climate change is to make drastic modifications immediately. It's too late to save the passenger pigeon and the vaquita porpoise and the northern white rhino. It's too late to save fossil fuel CEOs and the politicians who feed off them. Let's get some fresh DNA in office leading the renewable wave of the only future in which humanity has a chance to evolve.

# An Air Freshener for the Outhouse

People want to export more coal, drill for more oil, frack for more gas, all in the name of "producing more jobs at home."

I have no doubt that doing all this would indeed create thousands of jobs. But producing a job isn't the same thing as doing something useful for people.

We could hire thousands of people across the country to cut down every tree in every city. Those jobs would feed families for a while, but they'd devastate our cities in return. And eventually, those jobs would still peter out.

We could also hire tens of thousands of people to pick up sledgehammers and break up every sidewalk in the country. That would feed multitudes of families. The unemployment rate would plummet.

Well, yes, but don't be ridiculous. That would be sheer destruction, just for the sake of a job.

I think you're starting to get the point.

"Yes, yes, yes, that's all fine and good, but if *we* don't build that coal terminal or drill that well, someone else will."

Fair enough. But just because *someone* will be making a profit from destroying the environment doesn't mean *we* have to do it. When the Mafia wants a hit on a rival, *someone* will take the job of hitman. But just because *someone* will become a murderer doesn't mean it has to be *me*.

Trying to recover from all the damage caused by water pollution and carbon emissions and other toxins will cost the country a great deal more than the short-term profits waiting to be made now. There will clearly be a day of reckoning, and it isn't that far off. Do we want to be the person history ridicules and abhors or the person society respects and thanks? Do you want to be Hitler or Gandhi? Lincoln or Stalin?

Or perhaps we don't care what anyone else thinks or feels, as long as we get our money?

If selling your body makes you a prostitute, what does selling your soul make you?

There are countless jobs that could be created right now to start repairing the damage that's already been done, and to develop green energy that will *have* to be developed sooner or later whether we like it or not. Those are real jobs, too.

Or we could sit back and do another "feasibility study" to try to guess what these current operations will do if continued or increased.

I have to wonder, though, don't we know already? We've had coal for two centuries. We've had oil and gas for quite some time, too. And the evidence is conclusive that they all wreak unbelievable havoc on the environment and all things that live on the Earth, including humans.

This debate is like asking if an air freshener will make going to the outhouse more pleasant. Perhaps it will. But it's still an outhouse.

And it's one thing to have an isolated outhouse twenty yards from the main house. It's another thing to convert our living room to an outhouse as well.

Green energy is like indoor plumbing, a much better solution than adding a large bucket of sewage to every room. The fact is that there's no way to eliminate the repercussions of our presence on the Earth, but we can at the very least minimize the negative effects and try to preserve our world not only for our children and grandchildren, but also for *their* children and grandchildren, and for all of the life that has a God-given right to live on this precious planet as well.

# Environmental Serial Killers

I remember when I was a child, I read an article that made an amazing claim. Scientists recorded the electrical activity in certain plants and performed an experiment that showed plants had "emotions." When several plants were brutally slashed in the presence of other plants, the electrical activity among the spectator plants spiked. Even afterward, whenever the "murderers" re-entered the room, the "witnesses" would show increased electrical activity.

Plants, I concluded, were living beings that deserved to be treated with respect.

But when I told a neighborhood boy about the article, he laughed and immediately ripped some leaves from a bush in my front yard. For years afterward, whenever he passed by, he'd rip leaves and branches off the plants in front of me and laugh.

I was certainly horrified by his actions but equally confused. Even if he didn't believe the article himself, he knew that I did, so why did he want to be so mean?

Unfortunately, I've seen the same scenario repeat itself over and over as I've grown up. Many right-wing Republicans, for instance, seem to take an inordinate satisfaction in cutting down forests inside national parks, in fighting anyone trying to save the polar bears or the whales or any other creature, in behaving like Holocaust-deniers by insisting there's no such thing as global warming, and fighting with all their might to stop efforts to control it.

They *like* watching people who care about the environment suffer.

Whether they experience the same enjoyment out of hurting plants and animals as the young boys do who kill neighborhood cats and then grow up to be serial killers, I don't know, but they undeniably enjoy watching other humans suffer.

If they think a Democrat will feel pain if a wetland is destroyed, then they'll help that destruction come about by blocking efforts to save it. They have no particular animosity toward wetlands, of course. They simply have a pathological dislike for "their enemies" (i.e., their neighbors).

How the environment, which affects both liberals and conservatives equally, has become such a polarized issue is mystifying. Republicans could claim the issue as easily as anyone else. But since Democrats seem to have emphasized it first, rather than work together, God forbid, on this one single issue, Republicans have made it a vendetta to oppose any environmental protections they can.

I don't understand it. Even now, they could run with this topic still more strongly than Democrats (who, God knows, don't do nearly enough to protect the environment themselves) and turn it into their own cause, but the desire to hurt other people is simply too strong.

They *must* fight conservation efforts because they so desperately want to hurt their "opponents." If it means they kill off hundreds of other species to do it, then so be it. If it means drought and famine for our grandchildren, and even in our time for those useless people in Third World countries, so be it. What's important is to make a Democrat suffer, whatever the cost.

Perhaps we deserve to make ourselves extinct. We seem to be a despicable species at times. It's just a shame that as we destroy ourselves, we bring down so many other innocent lives with us.

Can plants really tell when there are murderers present? I don't know. But *I* can certainly tell. And watching the sadistic glee of these environmental serial killers both saddens and appalls me.

But just as Nazism ended and Germans became respectable citizens again, I cling to the hope that murderers of the environment will come around eventually as well.

# Murderers of Old Men

I remember reading a tragic news article once about two men, aged 102 and 99, who were shot to death while attending the funeral of their friend, who'd died at 100. It seemed more unfair than just the average terrible murder. To kill someone who'd made it so far seemed not only a crime against them but also a crime against humanity, a crime against nature itself.

But I feel this same sense of injustice whenever I read of someone logging unprotected redwoods, trees that have been fighting the odds for 500 years or more to live out their lives. What kind of person could kill a 500-year-old tree?

For that matter, just logging in an "average" old-growth forest, with trees merely 100 or 150 or 200 years old still seems to me a crime.

Of course, we can't do away with logging altogether. Not even an avid environmentalist could advocate that.

But we can certainly agree not to log in our national forests, and we can agree to rely more on tree farms than virgin forests.

When I went to the Muir Woods near San Francisco for the first time, I had two simultaneous, overwhelming impressions. First, of course, was a sense of awe being in the presence of life that had been thriving since even before my ancestors came to this country in 1650. Many of those trees had lived throughout my entire lifetime, and the lifetime of my father, and of his father, and his father, and his father, and back several more generations beyond that.

What kind of person does it take *not* to be overwhelmed with a sense of respect for a life like that?

But my other deeply felt impression that day was one of dismay. The Muir Woods covered an extremely small area, a few measly acres among what were previously many countless acres of these trees.

It's not that I only appreciate nature and shrug my shoulders at civilization. When I went to Paris, I was equally impressed with the art in the Louvre, the gothic Notre Dame, and with Sainte Chapelle, a church built almost 800 years ago which still to this day has never developed a single crack because it was so well constructed.

Anything that has survived so long deserves respect and preservation.

But when it involves an actual life, how can we dismiss it so carelessly?

Trees are not humans. They're not even an animal species. But they are alive, and even if they weren't an indispensable part of the ecosystem, they deserve to live out their lives naturally, at least as much as our industrial society can allow.

I eat beef, so I understand one life living off another. Even vegetarians eat plants and so live off other lives, too. It's impossible not to kill some members of other species to maintain our own lives. And trees are certainly no exception.

But there are alternatives to clear-cutting the land. There are alternatives to destroying old-growth forests.

We can live at least a little more fully in harmony with nature than we do now. All environmentalists are asking is that we make an effort.

Or are we really the type of person who can shoot a 102-year-old man and let it have no effect on our conscience? It's an important question.

I'm hoping deep down that we're better than the murderers of old men.

# God Himself Couldn't Burn This Planet…But Human Hubris Can

What will it take?

First-graders shot in the head at Sandy Hook didn't lead us to make even minimal gun regulations. Neither did children mutilated so badly in Uvalde they had to be identified by their DNA.

Will we need thousands of people to die of heatstroke this summer in the U.S. for us to create climate-focused policies? Will another entire town need to be destroyed by wildfires? Will it take a Category 5 hurricane with the highest storm surge ever to strike Miami or Charleston or New York?

Will even that not be enough for us to do more than offer lip service to the problem?

I'm afraid the only way to save the rest of the country, the rest of the planet, or, really, even a portion of it, is if "the public" finally realizes beyond a shadow of a doubt that the climate crisis is real.

Many Christians believe that God destroyed the world the first time through a global flood and that he'll do it a second time with fire. But it isn't God who's destroying the world. It's spoiled humans whose Heavenly Father seems to let them do whatever they want, no matter how irresponsible.

Humans sometimes behave responsibly eventually, but it's almost always too late for people they've harmed to benefit.

Most communities won't put up a stoplight at a troublesome intersection until a child is run over.

NASA wouldn't fix an acknowledged problem with its O-rings until the space shuttle Challenger exploded shortly after take-off.

Every day on my way to work in south Seattle, I pass dozens and dozens of Boeing 737 MAX planes stored on employee parking lots. Over 500 of the jets are out of commission worldwide as Boeing works to fix a software problem it admits knowing about over a year before the first of two crashes that killed 346 people. Even the first crash wasn't enough to spur them to address the problem.

Our knee-jerk reaction is to think that city councils and NASA and Boeing are run by terrible people, but really their behavior is normal. As humans, we simply don't like to believe the situations we find ourselves in are bad until we are forced to face them in undeniable ways.

Unfortunately, that means we must accept the deaths of thousands from heat stroke, the obliteration of entire towns, the loss of billions of dollars from storm and drought damage, before we'll do what must be done.

It would be far cheaper and less deadly to deal with problems up front, but humans are gamblers by nature, even though we all know the house always wins. Sometimes, we stop placing bets before we're bankrupt, and sometimes, we don't.

I'm not sure there's a way to skip a step in this process of denial and get right to the problem-solving part.

Humans will have no choice but to address the climate crisis on a local, national, and global level. The science is not debatable. It's the psychology that is.

How much are we willing to lose before we as a species are collectively ready to accept reality?

Promoters of the White Star Line boasted in 1912 that the *Titanic* was so well built "even God himself couldn't sink this ship." And God *didn't* sink that ship. Arrogant men who thought they were more powerful than Nature sunk that ship.

How do we interact meaningfully with leaders who actively work to keep us in denial until all five hundred 737 MAX planes plummet to the earth? Is it okay to encourage people to accept even just twenty more crashes?

The temperature reached a record 114 degrees F in France in June of 2019. It reached an all-time high of 90 in Anchorage, Alaska a few days later.

Not even the most radical eco-activists would try to "help" by deliberately creating problems, but surely we must be aware that foreign or domestic terrorists have access to matches. At least a few have access to surface-to-air missiles that could be used to knock out the power grid of a major city during the height of a heatwave. Or damage our water infrastructure.

The dangers are real, with or without additional malice.

It's difficult to find an AC left to buy in the midst of a heatwave, difficult even to find a fan. Forget about generators.

Do we plan ahead or wait until nothing's left?

Maybe we can just catch a plane to someplace cool and deny reality a bit longer. I hear the melting glaciers of Greenland are nice this time of year.

# Organic Water, Clean Natural Gas, and Giftwrapped Garbage

A television commercial the other day displayed a bottle labeled "Organic Water." Naturally, this gave me pause, as by definition, organic compounds must contain at least one carbon molecule. And there's no C in $H_2O$.

Looking more closely, I realized that in this case, "Organic" was part of the branding, not a description of the water itself. Still, it was hard not to feel misled. Organic water *sounds* healthy.

Greta Thunberg, the young Swedish climate activist, said that one of our biggest obstacles in addressing the climate crisis is that too many of us might be deceived by the spin oil and gas companies put on their "efforts" to limit carbon emissions. A couple of years ago, some fossil fuel corporations began airing commercials touting "clean" natural gas. More spin soon followed.

Burning fossil fuels is never clean, and since so much of the natural gas we use is extracted via fracking, we must also consider the millions of gallons of water permanently contaminated each day by the process.

There's no such thing as clean coal, either.

We've all heard the story about an enterprising man frustrated by a long garbage strike who put his household refuse in a box every day, giftwrapped it, and then slapped a bow on top. He would place the "gift" in the back seat of his car, park at a shopping center, and leave the car door unlocked. When he would return to his car later, he'd happily discover that his garbage was now someone else's problem.

While the story is likely apocryphal, this is essentially the same strategy used by fossil fuel corporations, only they are getting paid to foist *their* garbage on *us*. Over 550 toxic coal ash ponds are some of the permanent gifts that residents near coal mines are privileged to enjoy.

Climate scientists keep pointing out that while global warming will increase rainfall in some areas, often that extra rain will descend in downpours so heavy they'll cause catastrophic flooding. Other areas will see significantly less rain. The Sahara, we should remember, was once a large, verdant region of Africa until the last period of rapid climate change.

A recent study in *Nature Geoscience* reveals that almost 150 million trees were killed in California between December of 2011 and March of 2019 as a result of drought combined with higher temperatures. While that's a staggering number, we should realize it isn't a *final* number. More droughts and increasingly higher temperatures, both consequences of accelerating climate change, plus the resultant increase in wildfires every year, will keep killing more and more trees. The number won't stop at 150 million. Or 200 million. Or 250 million.

In *The Day after Tomorrow*, the character played by Dennis Quaid tells a group of politicians that an iceberg the size of Rhode Island just broke off an ice sheet. Currently, in Antarctica, the Thwaites ice sheet, the size of Florida, is collapsing. That's in addition to the thirty-five gigatons of ice a year we've lost between 2009 and 2017.

But we don't have to wait for cataclysmic sea level rise before we start experiencing serious water crises. Many of those toxic coal ash ponds gifted to us by fossil fuel companies overflowed during Hurricane Florence's assault on the Carolinas in 2018. Over fifty lagoons filled with pig waste overflowed as well.

I'm not sure we *want* organic water.

The Cuyahoga River in Ohio has caught fire several times from industrial debris and oil slicks in its waters.

Tap water near many fracking sites is easily ignitable.

In 1982, my first partner's grandmother heard an explosion near her home in Kenner, Louisiana. She ran outside into a heavy downpour, terrified to see the rain all about her ablaze. She didn't realize a plane had just crashed. She thought she was witnessing the end of the world.

It's essentially what we're all witnessing today. Oh, there will certainly be species that survive the current mass extinction event. We might even be among them.

In books and movies about nuclear war, there are always human survivors. But few of them ever seem very happy. We face a similarly hellish future across much of our planet if we don't begin taking drastic action now.

We can't giftwrap trillions of gallons of contaminated water.

We can't call water organic just because it contains carbon molecules from fossil fuels.

We can't irrigate our drought-stricken agricultural regions with water crammed full of lethal chemicals.

But if we're lucky, we can have our children's bodies treated with organic embalming fluids before we dig a hole in the hard-baked ground to hide their coffins.

# Climate Crisis Threatens the Mormon Church

While the devastating effects of the climate crisis will help fulfill prophecies about the terrors of the "last days," that's about the only benefit the Mormon Church will receive from them. Virtually every other effect will weaken the Church.

Members of The Church of Jesus Christ of Latter-day Saints often feel they're given special protection by Heavenly Father, despite scriptures claiming God is "no respecter of persons." In almost every account of natural disaster, we hear about how "the chapel was miraculously spared," "no missionary was harmed," or some other such claim. The truth, though, is that Mormons are increasingly impacted by the effects of worldwide climate crisis, both at home and abroad.

Scientists have determined that as global temperatures rise, so does sea level. Storms become more frequent, and because upper level steering currents are disrupted by climate change, even small storms can linger over an area and cause widespread devastation. In 2017, flooding impacted roughly 1400 Peruvian Latter-day Saints.

That same year, Hurricane Harvey dumped over five feet of rain and flooded six LDS meetinghouses in the Houston area, causing minor damage to another twenty. 800 homes of church members were damaged, with 2800 members displaced. Even the Houston temple was flooded.

In 2018, Hurricane Florence in the Carolinas flooded the homes of 20 members. Cyclone Gita seriously damaged a ward meetinghouse in Tonga as well as the Liahona high school there. Over in Samoa and American Samoa, Gita flooded the LDS Service Center and damaged the stake center in Pago Pago.

Just a few years earlier, Typhoon Haiyan destroyed the homes of hundreds of church members. According to the *Deseret News*, "In one Mormon congregation alone, 95 percent of the members saw their homes destroyed. Scores had lost family members, many carried out to sea with the current, never to return."

At least two ward meetinghouses were destroyed by Hurricane Katrina in 2005. Many displaced members in Louisiana and Mississippi moved out of the area permanently.

In 2016, an LDS stake center in Denham Springs, Louisiana was submerged when a storm stalled over the Baton Rouge area for days.

In 2008, Nauvoo was threatened by floods in the American Midwest. In 2019, the town was flooded. The Mormon Bridge connecting Nebraska and Iowa was washed away.

Extreme weather events caused by global warming are becoming more common around the world. They affect everyone, and since Mormons are part of "everyone," they affect members of the Church as well. Even those who don't lose their homes (or their lives) are impacted when FEMA and other government agencies use billions in taxpayer dollars to address disaster after disaster after disaster.

In 2017, members of the Mormon Church lost 150 homes in 16 California wildfires in Santa Rosa, Napa, Ukiah, Auburn, and Coffey Park. A mission home, a meetinghouse, and an Institute building were threatened. They survived the fires that year, but the Church will need to deal with more and more losses as wildfires in the west worsen in the coming years.

In 2018, 20 member families lost homes in the Carr fire near Redding, California. One can look up stark images of wildfires burning behind the Payson temple in Utah.

And who can forget the devastation wreaked upon members in Paradise that year? Two meetinghouses burned to the ground, the fire so intense that a metal beam supporting the roof of one melted. Almost every member in town, over 60 families, lost their homes.

These are no longer isolated incidents. This is the future of life on Earth as the climate crisis worsens and we continue refusing address it.

It bears remembering that all these disasters also impact the missionaries serving there at the time and disrupt missionary work in the area for years afterward.

Of course, nothing is *all* bad. Even climate crisis has a silver lining for Mormons. Temple work, in those temples that survive, will receive a boost, given the increased opportunity to perform baptisms for the dead.

Kinda gives "Jesus wants me for a sunbeam" a rather different meaning, doesn't it?

# If Climate Change Is Real but Not Caused by Human Activity, Don't We Still Need to Address It?

Of all the baffling comments climate change deniers make, the one that astounds me most is their admission that yes, climate change "appears" to be real, but it isn't caused by human activity.

Even if humans aren't responsible for causing climate change, we're still going to do something about it, right? If scientists discovered that an asteroid was heading for Earth and would cause global destruction, are you saying that as long as it hadn't been sent on that collision course by humans, you wouldn't want to deflect it?

Many devout Christians believe that the Second Coming is imminent, and Jesus will fix everything when he arrives. To address climate change on our own would imply that we don't trust God to take care of us.

But God could conceivably perform some miracle right now to bring people to him. So are Mormon missionaries preaching in Italy, and Baptists preaching in Guatemala, and Catholics preaching in Kenya implying that God can't take care of saving souls himself?

Despite the Amish opposition to electricity, and the opposition of Jehovah's Witnesses to blood transfusions, and that of Christian Scientists to medicine in general, most Christians have no problem accepting medical treatment or taking advantage of combustible engines or computers or any other scientific or technological advance.

So why do we draw the line at using science to solve a crisis that's already creating devastating floods and fires and famines at an ever-increasing pace? Especially when we know our refusal to act will only make our lives exponentially more miserable later?

Part of it is the sunk cost fallacy. We've put a great deal into the status quo, and changing things will be so difficult and costly that it's easier to pretend the responsibility is someone else's, not ours.

But time and effort and money aren't the real issues, at least not for most voters fighting climate action. For them, the overriding reason they won't support Green New Deal candidates is that to do so would cause them to lose face.

This refusal to address a global climate crisis is the natural result of people trying to protect their fragile egos. But I'm not saying that disparagingly. This is a normal human reaction. The phrase "cutting off your nose to spite your face" didn't come out of nowhere.

When I tested positive for HIV, I dreaded the day I had to tell my family because I knew what it would mean. They'd express sympathy, but they'd do it with a gleam in their eye, feeling vindicated that God had punished me for leaving the

Mormon Church. Painful as it was, I did tell them. Perhaps they didn't need to know, but I needed to live an honest life.

Opponents of fracking bans as well as bans on all new drilling and pipelines can convince themselves they're saving face through their opposition, but the thing is, the people they want to deceive can already see through them.

Four decades ago, one of my fellow missionaries wrote home weekly about all his incredible callings out in "the field." He told his friends and family he was a district leader, then a zone leader, then an assistant to the mission president. He did this even knowing that upon his arrival home, the bishop of his congregation would read a letter from the mission president specifying each position he'd actually held.

My missionary colleague *knew* a day of reckoning was coming, but he kept lying anyway, because the benefits of lying were immediate while the consequences of being found out would only occur later.

Climate change is real. Whether or not it's caused by human activity, it's an existential crisis we must address. Climate change activists must not rub their "rightness" in the face of those we're trying to enlist. And climate change deniers need to accept their lumps and do the right thing.

Humiliation isn't fatal. But if we don't act now, there may be no plastic surgeons left the day we're ready to have them build the new noses we'll need.

# Our Climate Loan Has Come Due

We took out an environmental loan by using fossil fuels even after understanding the havoc they were causing. We've fallen behind on our payments, and now the lender is demanding we settle our debt in full.

When I started my Biology degree, I didn't have much money. I'd paid for my BA in English with money I inherited from my mother. I paid for my MA in English by teaching a few composition classes in exchange for tuition. I managed to pay for my MFA while I took classes as well.

But I had to take out student loans to pursue my Biology degree. I was warned repeatedly to take out as little as possible because I'd have to pay it all back one day. "Be careful," I was told. "Be smart." "Think ahead." "There will be a day of reckoning."

But I took out the max allowed every semester. I was paying the rent and utilities and everything else by myself. I still needed a full income even while attending school. I *couldn't* "be smart." I *couldn't* think of the future. I was trying to get through this month's bills. I hoped to get a good job upon graduation. Or maybe I'd win the lottery. Somehow, I'd find a way to deal with the debt later.

I owed $48,000 by the time I graduated. That was nineteen years ago. I didn't get a good job. I didn't win the lottery. I still owe almost $18,000 despite making payments every month. It was only about a year ago that I was five days late for the first time, and the lender raised my interest rate as a penalty. Permanently.

We've long known that using fossil fuels was going to cause devastation down the line. But we needed electricity to run our refrigerators. We needed gasoline to get to work. We knew we'd regret it one day, but we were so overwhelmed by our immediate needs that we couldn't let ourselves worry about the future.

I can include my mortgage payment in bankruptcy proceedings if I need to. I can include my car loan. I can include my credit card.

But I can't include my student loan. I *have* to pay that whether I want to or not. And if I refuse, the lender can garnish my wages. There's no escaping that debt.

Progressive policy changes on tuition and student loan debt might eventually help students, but even the most progressive policy changes on fossil fuels cannot erase the debt we owe to the planet.

Student loans are crippling. I knew they would be and took them out anyway. So perhaps we can forgive ourselves for being foolish about our use of fossil fuels. But like it or not, our environmental loan has come due and we must repay it. The interest rate is already high, but the lender can—and will—raise it even higher if we don't pay immediately.

The human mind is capable of creating lovely sonnets. It's capable of studying epibatidine. We're smart and creative. But we're also good at denial. Like a man who knows his husband is cheating on him but who can pretend it isn't true as long as the words aren't said out loud, we can know and not know something essential at the same time. We've long understood there would be a day of reckoning for our use of fossil fuels. We said we'd deal with it then.

That then is now.

# Öl Macht Frei

My father was a tractor pull champion. A homebuilder by trade, his office walls were lined with dozens of shiny trophies. He was Texas state champion in his category. When he retired from building, he moved back to his farm, converting one field to a staging area where he could host his own tractor pulls. This was fun for him. It was validating. He was able to socialize, make some money, and feel important.

What's wrong with any of that?

Not much, really, except that each tractor could burn through an entire tank of gas in minutes.

Fossil fuel corporations are our biggest adversary in transitioning to other forms of energy that release less carbon into the atmosphere, but the biggest obstacle in getting "the people" to take those corporations down is the impact on our personal lives. My nephew works for an oil company and has been able to provide a comfortable living for his family for the past fifteen years. A smart guy, he never graduated from high school. The only job I remember him working before his current position was one painting cars. He also likes tractor pulls.

My nephew has several children he loves deeply. Each day he goes to work, he's condemning them to a harsher and harsher future. But he won't stop because to do so would put them in dire circumstances *today*.

Back when I was Mormon, my bishop worked for Shell Oil as a geologist. I'd long enjoyed geology, but he pointed out that it was difficult to earn money as a geologist unless you were searching for oil. That didn't particularly appeal to me, even in the days before I heard about global warming.

My bishop eventually became my stake president and presided over my Court of Love where I was excommunicated for being gay. As he pulled me into a separate room away from the group of high priests who'd convicted me, he said, "I know some great guys at work who are gay. I don't know why the Church has this position, but I don't have any choice but to excommunicate you."

Good people do terrible things because they feel they don't have options. We'll be unable to persuade the public to go along with the disruptive changes required not only to reduce carbon emissions but also to recapture tons of it already released. That means we must take a multi-issue approach.

Tuition-free college and trade school would help workers shift to new careers. But my nephew would't be able to attend any educational program two to four or six years without being able to provide for his family in the meantime. We need an adequate stipend for the time it takes folks to shift to other jobs.

We need guaranteed childcare as well. And no one's going to leave a secure position if they have to worry about medical bills. We can't cut our dependence on fossil fuels unless we implement single-payer or some other form of universal healthcare.

Our survival depends on a sweeping overhaul of our entire culture and economy. It's daunting. Deep into the world's sixth mass extinction event, the only one caused by human activity, we've just seen another sobering report on global warming. An additional million species will soon be added to the already staggering death toll.

Many brave souls fought against the Nazi regime, but many more did not, afraid that fighting back would guarantee their deaths while waiting it out might give them a chance to survive. The sign above the entrance to Auschwitz promised that work would make them free. They clung to the promise, even as they marched to the gas chambers.

The entrances to all fossil fuel companies, their storage facilities, and the work sites that process or transport those fossil fuels should have new signs erected over them.

"Öl macht frei."

Unless we can offer those who make their living bringing death to the world a viable alternative, they'll keep doing their jobs. Blaming them for their short-sightedness is both unfair and unhelpful. If we really want to save ourselves, we can't tackle this challenge one piece at a time.

A sizable chunk of the funds necessary to implement these radical changes can be requisitioned from the massive fossil fuel subsidies and tax breaks we currently give to fossil fuel corporations. The rest can be redirected from our bloated military budget.

Jews in Sobibor tasked with disposing of the bodies of their fellow captives finally reached an epiphany. Over 167,000 people had already been murdered there. Only a few hundred still remained in a concentration camp that was clearly being 100% liquidated. There was no more option of waiting it out.

As a group, they planned a mass escape. Most of them were killed in the attempt, but roughly fifty men survived. Fifty people out of an entire concentration camp full of people.

Their other option was never to fight back at all.

Since 1945, we've dreaded what World War III would look like. Well, it's here. The entire planet is facing an enemy greater than we've ever known. And it will take a massive, multi-faceted attack to achieve victory.

# The Climate Crisis Is World War III

World War I left twenty million people dead across the globe, more than half of them civilians. World War II killed between seventy and eighty-five million more, 3% of the world's population. Between fifty and fifty-five million of those deaths were civilians.

What kind of death toll lies ahead if there is ever a World War III?

We'll find out soon enough, as the third world war is already underway.

*A Planet Called Treason* was my first Orson Scott Card novel. I loved how the title offered the reader multiple meanings. On the one hand, the planet in question is named Treason, like our planet is named Terra. But Card, a devout Mormon, provided his planet with a spirit, the way Mormon theology insists the Earth has a spirit of its own, separate from the spirits inhabiting all the various life forms on and below its surface. When the planet in the novel is betrayed by the actions of its villains, the planet calls out "Treason!" through the way it reacts.

Most of the wars in mankind's past have pitted humans against each other. But now humans have declared war on the planet itself. Not just the climate but the soil, too. The planet isn't fighting back, as in Card's novel, so much as allowing its attackers to shoot themselves in the foot and step on their own land mines.

In Michael Moore's documentary *Fahrenheit 11/9*, we see a clip of a young Asian woman concentrating on her phone. "'This is not a drill,'" she reads the text alert she's just received. "Oh, my god!" She looks at her partner in stunned confusion. "What do we do?"

For twenty minutes on January 13, 2018, the people of Hawaii desperately tried to reach their loved ones as they mistakenly believed they faced almost certain death from an incoming nuclear missile. In our current political climate, the threat of a devastating global war, which had mostly lain dormant since the end of the Cold War, now hangs over our heads once again.

The last world war was so catastrophic that we've repeatedly tried to imagine what World War III would look like. Movies such as *The Day After*, *Red Dawn*, *Dr. Strangelove*, and *War Games* helped us prepare to survive or prevent such a calamity.

But despite all the forethought, we were still blindsided.

The climate crisis is a far larger threat than the Kaiser ever was, a more dangerous threat than the Nazis could ever dream of being, a more powerful threat than the Soviet Union or China or any other political or military entity. We can rebuild Berlin or Hiroshima or Beirut or Atlanta.

We can't rebuild an entire planet.

In the coming decades, almost 600 coastal cities around the world, housing an estimated 800 million people, will face permanent inundation or repeated heavy storm surges from increasingly severe hurricanes and cyclones.

That's just the damage along the coastlines.

The Vietnam War lasted two decades. The War of the Roses lasted thirty-two years. The Spanish conquest of the Inca Empire took place over forty years. The Hundred Years' War actually dragged on for 116 years. The *second* Hundred Years' War lasted 126.

The cost of rebuilding or relocating homes, businesses, factories, farms, and people during World War III will likely dwarf spending from all previous wars combined. Right-wing conservatives will look back with nostalgia to the times when immigrants and refugees only numbered in the low millions. Ancient, deadly pathogens released from the ice or permafrost will almost certainly contribute to even further suffering.

Anne Frank wasn't officially executed during World War II. She died of disease that proliferated because of conditions created during the war.

Terra isn't going to die. Probably 10-15% of the species still alive today will survive as well. And not all deaths during a conflict happen at the beginning.

That doesn't mean we aren't at war right now.

The gas chambers we're being led to today are filled with a gas just as deadly as the hydrogen cyanide-based gas used during the Holocaust. Just as deadly as the mustard gas used in the first world war.

We've thought about World War III for seventy-five years, but we don't have to wonder if or when it will begin any longer. The only relevant question now is how we're going to win this ultimate War of the World.

And whether we'll ever be lucky enough to face World War IV.

# My Mother's Forced Abortion and Sterilization

When my sister was pregnant with her first child back in 1976, we teased her with the movie *It's Alive!* in which a mutant baby with claws and fangs kills the entire medical team that helps deliver it within moments of its birth.

My sister and I didn't realize at the time that *we* were the killer offspring. My best friends were killer offspring. My Sunday School teachers were killer offspring. My Mormon bishop, who worked for an oil company, was a major killer offspring.

For a nation that seems to be increasingly pro-life, we seem to have no problem aborting the offspring of virtually every other life form.

The majority of Americans are urban dwellers or, at their most rural, suburbanites. We visit parks or grow a few flowers in our front yard, maybe a vegetable or two in a window box, but for the most part, we've lost our connection to nature: continually pregnant with new life—spring buds, fruiting blackberry bushes, robins laying eggs, cows calving, corn ready to harvest for eating or for gathering seeds for the next generation.

On a single visit to a conservatory greenhouse, I overheard three different people ask a gardener, "Are those grapes?" while pointing to a fishtail palm tree with its cluster of seeds. Do we not even know what grapes look like anymore? Or grapevines?

Many Americans who are adamantly pro-life when it comes to human fetuses are fine with aborting the life Mother Nature attempts to bring into the world. We clear cut old growth forests to establish palm oil plantations to flavor our chips. We block salmon breeding grounds with dams. We hunt whales to extinction. We blithely continue using pesticides we know kill bees. Once those bees are gone, hundreds of plant species that depend on them will join their fate within a single pollinating season. And when those plants go, so do the essential foods human rely on to fill our plates…and bellies.

When we hear about a teenage girl abandoning her newborn in a dumpster, we're ready to burn her at the stake. If the death of that baby qualifies as infanticide rather than abortion, the problem is that many pro-life activists conflate the two all the time. Pro-life lawmakers force women to hold burials for miscarried fetuses. Abortion is compared to the Holocaust. Over 60 million abortions have been performed in the U.S. since Roe v. Wade. That makes pro-choice voters worse than Nazis.

The direct human death toll from the Exxon Valdez oil spill, the Deepwater Horizon spill, and dozens of others can't possibly compare to death camp totals. But do the lives of the 250,000 birds, the loss of billions of salmon and herring eggs, and the countless other animals killed when the Valdez left

1300 miles of coastline covered in oil count? Do the lives of the one million birds and hundreds of thousands of other animals killed by the BP oil spill count? Does the incalculable number of lives lost in the 1000+ other oil spills in the U.S. count? Those killed in oil spills around the rest of the globe?

An oil train derailed in Lac-Mégantic in the province of Quebec, Canada, burning half the downtown and leaving forty-seven people dead. All but three of the surviving downtown buildings had to be demolished because of petroleum contamination. Over 1200 people were killed by a series of pipeline explosions in Nigeria. I hope the thousands of coal miners killed in dozens and dozens of mine disasters count for something, too.

We're horrified by the ethical implications of using stem cells harvested from aborted fetuses to develop cures for diseases that affect the rest of us. We're conflicted when parents choose to bring another child into the world for the primary purpose of providing a bone marrow transplant for their already-born daughter.

But are we concerned about the ethics of fracking? Over 250 *billion* gallons of water have been permanently contaminated in the U.S., and the number increases by twenty-five million more gallons *every day*.

Is that the action of a pro-life lawmaker? A pro-life political party? A pro-life religion? A pro-life nation?

Leading pro-life activists are so concerned about the accidental loss of a fetus that an Alabama woman whose pregnancy was terminated by the five bullets an attacker fired at her faces years in prison for precipitating an "abortion" by starting the argument that led to the shooting.

Will there be any jail time for the fossil fuel CEOs and shareholders who created a climate where wildfires tear through California towns and Greek villages and Israeli forests, killing hundreds?

Will there be manslaughter charges for the ship captains and train engineers and truck drivers who transport the oil and gas and coal killing both humans and members of countless other species in ferocious storms, devastating droughts, and cataclysmic floods? How about for those in management who send those captains and drivers and engineers out overworked and carrying too much cargo?

Who goes to prison for widespread crop losses?

Who goes to prison for rising sea levels that cause billions in property damage and lead to higher death tolls from more frequent storm surges?

Pro-life voters are horrified by forced abortions in China and North Korea and the sterilization of nonconsenting women in the U.S. over many decades, while with a religious zeal we accept the forced destruction of our planet and most of the life on it, witnessing first-hand the sixth mass extinction event in planetary history.

Pro-life activists *say* they don't approve of radicals who have shot abortion clinic nurses, murdered abortion doctors in their churches, and bombed abortion clinics. But their rhetoric insists that every avenue for stopping the slaughter of innocents must be pursued.

Will those of us who accept the reality of scientific findings be forced to target fossil fuel workers or CEOs or shareholders? Will we be forced to bomb oil tankers and storage facilities and wells?

If we do, can we claim self-defense? Those killing doctors insist they're saving the unborn. But if a pro-life activist can worry about a bean-sized clump of cells, why can't we worry about the billions of humans already here? Why can't we worry about the hundreds of trillions of other living beings?

Why can't we worry about the life that bean-sized clump of cells will face once forced into the world?

We're defending not only the unborn of all species but defending ourselves as well. We're the ones who die when the air quality in our major cities hits critical levels during weeks of wildfires. We're the ones who die in those wildfires, and in historic floods, and in ever-worsening heat waves. Over one hundred and ten thousand died in Europe and western Russia during the 2003 and 2010 heat waves. In June of 2019, France hit an all-time record high for any day ever—114.6 F.

And summer had barely begun.

CEOs of fossil fuel corporations aren't abortion "providers." They are abortion enforcers.

If pro-life activists are so concerned about the abortion of human fetuses that they'll back people like Donald Trump, how concerned are *we* about the crisis of climate abortion?

If those on the right are conflicted by the terrorist actions of their colleagues against abortion providers, those on the left who are even more pro-life are still more horrified. So what's someone who wants to stop the abortions forced on Mother Nature to do?

We must at the very least take action on a social and financial level. If churches can excommunicate members of their congregation who perform abortions, we can shun every lawmaker who bans protests against fossil fuel companies, every fossil fuel secretary and salesperson, every fossil fuel CEO and shareholder.

We must petition our banks to stop funding pipelines and other fossil fuel infrastructure. We must change institutions if they won't.

We must demand our cities and universities divest from fossil fuels.

We can join climate strikes like the one scheduled for September 20.

If we're truly pro-life, if we want to remain a species Mother Earth won't *want* to abort, we must become the offspring that doesn't kill the moment we come out of the womb. Or the sequel to *It's Alive!* will be *We're All Goners!*

*Johnny Townsend*

# Dinosaurs Building the World's Largest Magnet

When we look back at the tragic end of the Age of Dinosaurs, we assume they were helpless victims of natural forces. But what if the dinosaurs brought their deaths upon themselves?

Humans boast of being the most intelligent species this planet has ever known. Understanding the cataclysmic event that wiped out the dinosaurs sixty-five million years ago, we make modest efforts to prepare for another large asteroid heading our way. We entertain ourselves with movies about destroying those dangerous objects before they strike the Earth, showing ourselves superior to those lumbering creatures who didn't know what hit them.

All the while actively seeking self-destruction.

We "harvest" our forests "sustainably," even though any seedling planted today will require two hundred years or more to reach the size of the tree being replaced. And that's in industrialized nations. In Brazil, the Amazon rainforest is being cut down faster than anyone can replant it, not even to harvest the wood but just to clear the land. Fires are deliberately set to clear even more. And the climate crisis has led to record numbers of "natural" wildfires—over 70,000—raging across the area, destroying one of the world's largest carbon sinks even more rapidly.

134

We cut down indigenous forests in southeast Asia to make way for palm oil plantations.

We tear up regulations that would help prevent the extinction of endangered species, even knowing we're in the midst of a global mass extinction event.

We create and incorporate per- and polyfluoroalkyl substances (*PFAS*), even knowing they contaminate drinking water everywhere they're used. We continue to use pesticides that are not only linked to cancer but also wipe out bee populations, even knowing that bees are the sole pollinators for many plants essential to human welfare.

We develop nuclear weapons and cancel nuclear arms treaties. We develop biological and chemical weapons designed to kill millions of people at a time (and virtually every other lifeform living among them). We continue operating nuclear power plants, despite evidence they aren't safe from nature, much less from human fallibility and malevolence.

We refuse to end our dependence on fossils fuels, drilling new wells every day, fighting any legislation to curb our fossil fuel use, criminalizing protests by those who don't want to end up like the dinosaurs.

But because we keep adding more carbon to the atmosphere as quickly as we can, fully knowing the devastation it causes, we're active participants in our own self-destruction. We watch as Greenland's ice sheet melts faster than predicted. We watch as the ice in Antarctica melts. We watch as record heat waves kill hundreds of people, thousands, tens of thousands.

We watch as large corporations legally steal water around the world. Fracking, of course, continues unabated, permanently contaminating millions more gallons of groundwater every day.

We brush off the few political candidates who recognize the crisis and want to do something about it. We criticize and insult and lambast our friends who want to support those candidates.

It's like watching the most intelligent species of dinosaur develop the world's biggest magnet and point it toward the asteroid belt, deliberately attracting the largest iron-nickel objects they can find, boasting that they're about to create incredible new opportunities with all the precious metals they're bringing to the Earth.

# Let's Wear Shorts to Church!

What is considered proper or respectful or professional attire not only varies across cultures but also within the same culture over time. Given the enormity of the climate crisis, we must make common sense adaptations to our idea of what's "acceptable" if we hope to drastically lower our energy consumption. Let's start by wearing shorts to church.

In the past, almost every LDS priesthood leader sported a beard. "Mormon underwear" was one piece and extended to our ankles and wrists. We now wear two-piece garments that are significantly shorter and which have been modified in several other ways as well. Since the marks in the fabric are symbolic, we don't need the knee mark to rest precisely over the knee. Let's shorten garments even more to allow every endowed member to wear shorts and to allow women to wear sleeveless dresses. There's really no reason, of course, that fashion for men can't include sleeveless dress shirts as well. It's not blasphemy.

Knees are not sex organs. Neither are shoulders. Let's stop teaching our sons to swoon when they see them. Tackling the climate crisis means discarding "moral" obstacles that are detrimental both morally and physically.

Some professional workplaces already allow employees to wear shorts in the office, even to go barefoot. The building managers use less air conditioning in the summer—and therefore less fuel—but the employees are still comfortable enough to get their work done. If we're talking about 50,000 workplaces, or 10,000 churches, the benefits add up. It's something we can do now, without having to wait for innovations in technology.

When I was a missionary in Rome, the temperature could be quite warm by April. But the mission president insisted that no elder leave their apartment without a suit coat until *he* gave the order. By mid-May, we were all miserable, but the president was not ready to let us go out in our slacks and white shirts just yet. We had to suffer a little longer for propriety's sake.

Then, on May 16th, suddenly it was proper and respectable to walk around without a coat.

Even back then, the arbitrary nature of the decision struck me, all the more when I realized the sister missionaries had no such requirement. If they felt warm the first day of March, or even in mid-February, they didn't have to wear a jacket at all. Nowadays, sister missionaries can do the unthinkable—go without pantyhose and even wear pants, absolute and utter apostasy just a few years ago.

Businessmen often head to work these days without the ties that were formerly mandatory attire. We have "casual Friday" or "game day Friday" when professionals go to work in clothing that would have seemed shocking twenty or thirty years ago.

We must make similar adaptations at church. We need to wear heat-appropriate clothing. Eliminating ties alone would allow us to raise the thermostat a degree or two. Jesus never wore a tie. Ties aren't *essential* for showing God respect. And let's hear it for sandals at church. Jesus wore them even in the temple.

If Mormons want uniform ward meetinghouses and stake centers, we at least need to build them with architectural features that help regulate temperature. At a minimum, we can paint the roof of every church white.

If we can't lobby health insurance companies to cover sun block, let's make sure every member has access to it through the Bishop's Storehouse.

Church leaders are notoriously resistant to change, so while we wait for official word on possible adaptations, individual members need to start taking personal initiative incorporating these strategies on their own.

Perhaps we could also try a pilot program where one Sunday a month, all the meetings are conducted remotely. We could add a "gasoline fast day" where members are encouraged not to drive and to donate the money they would have spent on fuel toward helping retrofit the homes of members.

With a little thought, and perhaps some divine inspiration, we can develop other ways to make the cultural changes necessary to address the climate crisis. Obviously, wearing sandals isn't going to solve the problem by itself, but it's indicative of the shift in mindsets and worldviews that *is* necessary.

So let's start wearing shorts to church.

# Make Earth Great Again

I was the only person on light rail carrying a protest sign. Mine was pretty tame: "What have you got against a stable climate?" on one side, with "The climate crisis is World War III" on the other. A few passengers glanced nervously my way. Was I one of those crackpot preachers carrying warnings about the end of the world?

I wasn't far off, I suppose.

Fortunately, when I arrived at the Pioneer Square station just before 1:00 and stepped out into the transit tunnel, I spotted a couple of other people headed to the climate rally at City Hall.

We were deep below ground, and I noticed that both the first and second escalator were out of service, as was the elevator. Seattle's not a poor city. Were these machines left unrepaired due to a lack of employees? Or had someone deliberately delayed work to make it harder for protesters to reach City Hall? I recognized my suspicions were probably unfounded, but when elected officials so often oppose constructive action on climate, it's impossible not to wonder.

Old and fat, I was already exhausted by the time I reached street level and trudged slowly up a very steep James Street to 4th Avenue. But here I was heartened. A huge contingent of marchers was coming down James from First Hill. Already, every spot along the impressive staircase leading up to City Hall from the street was filled with protesters. The entire plaza beside it was filled as well. Not a single free spot was left on the sidewalk in front of the building.

The street itself had a good hundred or so protesters, but there was plenty of room to maneuver. I stood in the middle of 4th Avenue, in the middle of the block, and held up my sign, flipping it every few minutes so people both in front and in back could see both slogans. Lots of photographers were about, most amateur but some carrying professional equipment.

"Let's Care Harder" one sign encouraged.

"Don't be a fossil fool," chided another.

My husband Gary was supposed to be somewhere in the crowd. He was leading a small group from the Freedom Socialist Party and had started the day at 9:00 a.m. at Cal Anderson Park on Capitol Hill, where protesters rallied for three hours before starting their march downtown. I was grateful so many folks were present that I couldn't find him.

I wasn't up to standing for six or seven hours, and my diabetes made it impossible to go that long without a bathroom break. But I wanted my body to count at City Hall.

The Raging Trannies sang a few protest songs, followed by kids from the Sunrise Movement.

While the event was primarily a student strike, people of all ages milled about. I smiled when I realized another large surge of protesters was coming down James Street to join us. The crowd around me thickened. I couldn't quite see where the youth speakers were standing, talking about indigenous land and the effects of the climate crisis on all marginalized peoples, how action on climate was fundamentally tied to economic and racial justice. A balcony high above the plaza was filled with protesters and a man with large video equipment, but I saw no microphone or speakers.

When I still lived in New Orleans, my Mormon bishop had worked for Shell. I'd been interested in geology, but he'd told me the only way to make money with such a degree was to look for oil.

I studied Nathaniel Hawthorne instead and didn't make money.

I remembered waking up one night during my college days to a loud bang. When I climbed out of bed to investigate, I saw my father creeping down the stairs with a baseball bat. He thought someone had kicked in our front door.

An explosion at the Norco oil refinery fifteen miles away had killed seven workers and released 159 million pounds of chemical waste into the atmosphere.

Somewhere in front of me, I could hear students on the City Hall plaza introducing each other, a fifteen-year-old, a thirteen-year-old, some making hyperbolic statements that would offer easy opportunities for attacks by right-wing climate deniers. "The climate crisis isn't something in the future. It's right now! We'll be dead in three years!"

Or something along those lines. Even in worst case scenarios allowing for billions of deaths, still decades in the future, there would nevertheless be millions of survivors. But the student had the gist of the problem—it was serious and needed addressing.

One of the students asked the crowd not to photograph her or post pictures of her online, to protect her safety. It seemed melodramatic, until I remembered recent posts right-wing folks had made about Alexandria Ocasio-Cortez and Ilhan Omar.

"We're skipping our lessons to teach you one," read a sign making its way through the crowd.

The word "Greed" had its "d" crossed out on another sign, replaced with an "n."

Two young people walked by, wearing stickers on their shirts proclaiming, "I registered to vote today."

A huge surge of marchers joined us from Cherry Street to the north. 4th Avenue was getting quite crowded. I had a flashback to Mardi Gras day on Bourbon Street and began feeling trapped.

I still couldn't find Gary.

Some unseen person at the microphone led everyone in chants and singalongs. I was never able to participate in such things, instead nodding in agreement and waving my sign. Passersby looked at my scribbled slogans, none of them very impressed. I'd have to come up with something better for the next rally.

"Seas are rising," I read on one sign, "and so are we."

"Replant the forests," said another.

Hey! Gary's head moved along next to that sign. He was the one carrying it. The other side read, "Free mass transit."

Was it trapped?

Oh.

There were too many people between us for me to reach him.

Gary and I had just celebrated our twelfth anniversary a few days earlier, eating at a restaurant in our Rainier Beach neighborhood that had been a gas station in the 1940's, its façade made of round river stones. We'd had a great view of Lake Washington, but cars zoomed past through the entire meal, making it difficult to hear one another.

Gary had bought me light-blocking blinds for my home office. I'd bought him an energy efficient window for his. Our tiny house was 113 years old.

Another huge surge of protesters joined us from Cherry Street. Surrounded now by several hundred people, I squeezed my way to the sidewalk on the west side of the street and leaned against a plywood wall blocking off a huge excavation in the area below, space for a parking garage underneath the high-rise planned for the site.

"We've just been told the media are reporting 10,000 protesters here today!" another invisible person on the platform somewhere on the plaza announced.

As I'd left home earlier, I'd been afraid there might only be sixty or seventy people at the rally. But in a city of over a million, it was still disappointing a few more didn't show up. The superintendent of Seattle Public Schools had told all the students that if they skipped class to attend the climate strike, their absences would be considered unexcused.

And this in Seattle, a progressive city, in a state governed by Jay Inslee, whose presidential bid had been based on addressing the climate crisis.

"Make Earth Great Again" I saw on a new sign.

"We're HOT and bothered!" another read.

"My retirement plan isn't a 401k, it's 685 ppm of $CO_2$."

Tammy Morales, Shaun Scott, and Kshama Sawant, local leaders and candidates, spoke of their commitment to address the crisis. Kshama belonged to a different Socialist party than Gary did, but she was the boldest member on the city council. I received emails from her all the time on rent control and other issues important to residents being priced out of the city.

A cute young man, thirtyish, walked past me, handing out flyers on the importance of increasing link light rail service and adding a subway line now, not decades in the future. He hugged another young man he saw in the crowd.

Many gray-haired protesters were adding their energy, wearing buttons and T-shirts and hats with slogans. One carried a sign reading, "Make love, not $CO_2$," a message that probably resonated more with the older protesters than the hundreds of kids present.

A huge contingent of Amazon workers demanding their company do more to address the crisis milled about. I'd heard some Google workers were coming, too, but I couldn't clearly identify them. Many of the workers held signs demanding Amazon stop providing web services to fossil fuel companies. It took me a few moments to understand the "NO AWS FOR FOSSIL FUEL COMPANIES" signs. I'd thought they were asking me not to feel sorry for the demise of the fossil fuel industry. There was no danger of that.

Though I knew my nephew in Louisiana depended on a fossil fuel job to support his family. My cousin in Houston did, too.

Gary's white-haired head bobbed in the distance. He'd grown up Mormon as I had. We'd both volunteered two years of our lives as missionaries, in Rome of all places. We'd only met after I lost both my apartment and my job to Hurricane Katrina and been forced to relocate.

I wondered how many other climate change refugees were in the crowd today.

More were surely on the way, next year, and the year after, and the year after that. Hardly anyone in Seattle was even following the devastation Tropical Storm Imelda had just caused in eastern Texas the day before, forty inches of rain in some areas. Internal immigration from our own country was going to be devastating in the coming years, much less what was about to happen in other parts of the world.

A protester waved a sign off to my right. "Treat the world as if we plan to stay."

It was 2:12, and I was getting tired. A few other people had begun wandering off, and I decided to join them. If I waited much longer, downtown workers would pack the light rail, and getting home would be miserable. As it was, once I reached Rainier Beach, I'd have to compete with all the students who'd gone to class today, making the bus ride up the hill unpleasant.

Besides, I had to pee.

I walked down James and then descended several flights of stairs to the platform. Four or five other people with signs were also waiting to board. After finding a seat in the rear car, I casually positioned my sign so that other passengers could still read it as we headed south.

I just missed the 106 and didn't feel like waiting, so I carried my sign five blocks to Rainier Avenue. The 7 Prentice pulled up a few minutes later, a great bus if you could catch it, so close to the end of the line that only a handful of riders were still aboard. I could see the driver read one of my slogans as I stepped on. He looked me in the eyes and gave me a nod which I decided to interpret as approval.

I still had a five-minute walk from the closest stop to my house and, like the missionary I used to be, I continued to carry my sign high as I walked along Renton Avenue. Turning the corner when I reached my street, I saw Gary's truck in front of the house and smiled. He gave me a kiss when I walked in the door, and then we turned on the news. He was asleep within minutes, holding my hand as he always did while napping on the sofa.

Four million people had attended 2500 climate rallies in 185 countries in the past twenty-four hours. Some of the protest signs featured on the news segment included "Losing Nemo," with a dying clown fish painted next to the words. Another movie reference featured a poster showing several burning trees. "Run, Forest." Yet another sign read, "Yo mamma's so hot she's about to experience desertification and rising sea levels."

I hoped the youth would be able to spur grownups to act our age.

I hoped they'd get the job done even if the rest of us were too stupid or too lazy or too greedy to do it ourselves.

I watched as the news went to commercial, an ad for a major fossil fuel corporation appearing onscreen, an actor telling us what a responsible job the company was doing providing clean energy.

When Gary awakened a few minutes later, I squeezed his hand, kissed him on the cheek, and headed to the kitchen to start dinner.

# What if the Apocalypse Started and No One Cared?

A few days ago, a volunteer firefighter in Australia was killed when a fire tornado during one of the country's most catastrophic fire seasons lifted a fire truck and dropped it on him. While the fires raging over 15,000,000 acres have received plenty of attention, the relatively low number of human fatalities leads many people to shrug and move on to the next, more exciting, headline. We note what happened, but we don't really *do* anything about it.

What if the Apocalypse started and no one cared?

Fires recently swept across Siberia, across the Amazon rainforest, and in most other places routinely susceptible to wildfires. But this isn't "just the way life is."

Almost a billion animals have died so far in the most recent Australian wildfires. One can only imagine how many died in the Amazon. Warming oceans are killing just as much sea life, but those deaths are even further removed from our consciousness.

What must life have been like in Naples, the second largest city in Europe at the time, during the plague outbreak in 1656 that left 60% of its residents dead?

It's not as if humans haven't experienced overwhelming death tolls before. Outbreaks of plague killed up to a third of all humanity. The flu epidemic of 1918 killed fifty million people worldwide.

Is mass human death really what it's going to take for us to recognize the scale of the climate emergency?

Well, thanks to our inaction, we'll be getting it sooner rather than later. Perhaps not this year. Perhaps not next. But we should spend a moment thinking about it while we still have time to prepare.

How would we cope if three million New Yorkers died in the next year? A million farmers across the country? What would happen if a third of Microsoft employees died over the next few months? How would we manage if Jeff Bezos and 300,000 of his employees were wiped off the face of the Earth before the end of the year?

Humans have survived such extraordinary catastrophes before and will again. But if *you're* one of those 300,000 Amazon employees, wouldn't you *prefer* not to be a death others are strong enough to endure?

The overwhelming devastation of the Boxing Day tsunami which killed 230,000 people in the span of a few hours pales in comparison to what awaits us if we don't act decisively.

It isn't true, of course, to say "no one" cares. Lots of people care. Just not enough. Voters are still electing politicians devoted to supporting the fossil fuel industry. Even as Australia burns, its prime minister flies off for a vacation in Hawaii.

After okaying additional drilling on public lands, the U.S. president leaves on another golf excursion.

The Canadian PM tries to appear liberal and humane while doing everything in his power to expand fracking and tar sands projects.

The human species is not good at proactive problem solving. Even when we can see possible disasters looming, we often wait until *after* they take place before we accept the burden of addressing the underlying causes.

No one builds appropriate levees in New Orleans until after a thousand residents drown. No one fixes the obvious flaws in the 737 MAX until after two planes full of passengers crash. No one addresses problems with O-rings until a space shuttle explodes during lift-off.

It's simply the way humans are made.

If this is a genetic flaw, the principle of survival of the fittest may solve it without us. Often, though, there are cultural aspects to our sense of denial and apathy, and those are things we can address right now.

Religious leaders can stop teaching us to welcome the End of the World. Religious adherents can stop following leaders who won't. If there is a god, would he/she/it really be *mad* at you for trying to save the lives of your children?

As the Nazis swept across Europe, initiating a war that led to the deaths of tens of millions on that continent, and as Japanese soldiers swept across the Pacific, bringing death to millions more, they created a global disaster ending the lives of over seventy-five million people.

And even that will be a drop in the contaminated bucket in comparison to what awaits us if we keep postponing action.

But fear isn't a useful motivator. Neither are facts. So what will it take?

If the threat of economic ruin and agricultural collapse and the death of a billion people won't spur us to make necessary change, is the only option left to wait around until the promised threats materialize in full?

Perhaps it is. Maybe our reluctance to behave proactively truly is hard-wired and not a cultural artifact.

But when the soldiers of mass extinction come marching into town, let's hope for a French Resistance, let's hope for Dutch women who lure some of those soldiers to their deaths. Let's hope brave citizens of America and Britain and Norway and China and Mexico volunteer to take up arms.

If patriots are willing to protect freedom and democracy at all costs, perhaps it's worth noting that when civilizations collapse, freedom and democracy die with them.

Still, as heartbreaking as watching koalas burn to death may be, it's just not *fun* doing anything about it. It's much more entertaining to turn the channel and watch the latest idiocy perpetrated by our hated politician of choice.

If that gets old after a while, too, there's always a new episode of *Survivor* coming on soon. And when there's a commercial break, we can go to the bathroom and flush while we still have water.

# Drunks Don't Make the Rules Against Drunk Driving

Do we let drunks make the rules against drunk driving? Do we let heroin addicts make the rules regarding which drugs to legalize? Do we let pimps make the rules surrounding prostitution?

Then why do we trust corporations to make the rules on how to address the climate crisis? Or healthcare? Or anything else?

A meme circulating on social media recently pointed out an outrageous fact. If you made $5000 at work every day, and you worked seven days a week, would you feel reasonably satisfied with your income? Even Publishers Clearinghouse commercials only tempt us with "$5000 a week for life!" and most of us can barely dream about such riches. But what if we made that much money *every day*?

And what if we *never* took a day off? What if we made $5000 a day every day, every week, every month, for fifty years? What if we never took a sick day, never took vacation? What if we were somehow able to work even more than fifty years? *What if* we'd made $5000 a day every day since Columbus sailed to America in 1492, every day for over five centuries? Would we be satisfied with that level of income?

If we had made that much money for that length of time, we *still* wouldn't be billionaires. We'd *still* have less money than Jeff Bezos makes *in a week*.

Has no one in the past 500+ years had enough money to live a comfortable life?

None of us needs a billion dollars a week. And yet corporate leaders are never satisfied. They always want more. And more. They invest millions of dollars in politicians because they can reap hundreds of millions more in deregulation.

At this level, greed has become addiction.

Are we wise to allow addicts to make the rules about healthcare? Are we wise to allow addicts to make the rules determining how much toxic waste they can release into the environment? Are we wise to allow addicts to make the rules over whether to curb the carbon emissions that let them lead lives of addiction in the first place?

We don't let nurses addicted to opiates have the key to the narcotics box. We don't let child molesters work around children.

So why in the world do we trust corporate leaders and the politicians they support to have our best interests at heart? Even people who start off good and kind become untrustworthy when controlled by their addictions.

However much we personally benefit from the addictions of these people should not dictate our own response to policy, unless we've become addicts, too. I order products from Amazon. I Google subjects I want to read up on. I use Facebook to connect with friends. I use electricity and gas to function in society.

But I vote for candidates who refuse money from PACs and corporations. I vote for candidates who put the needs of the people over the needs of CEOs.

I don't do it out of principle, mind you. I do it because I don't want a kleptomaniac in control of my life savings.

Con artists are effective at persuading their marks that they aren't grifters. Addicts are skilled at hiding their addictions. But when we *know* how people are making their money and we support them anyway, we're reduced to lives as addicts ourselves, addicted to hype and spin, to lies and self-delusion.

So let's get ourselves into rehab, and let's stop allowing addicts to make the rules that lead us all to self-destruction.

# What the *Titanic* Teaches Us About the Climate Crisis

Okay, I admit it. I love the movie *Titanic*. Kate Winslet is the perfect heroine, an intriguing combination of vulnerability and strength. I love that she's a little heavier than the usual female lead. And her performance feels authentic.

But my enjoyment of the movie is seriously diminished every time Rose's fiancé Cal chases down her new love, Jack. The ship is taking on water, and all this idiot can think about is trying to shoot the dirt-poor artist. Then when Cal's bodyguard handcuffs Jack to a pipe below deck, I want to scream. The ship has only minutes before it meets its doom, and Jack is a steerage passenger. He has almost no chance of surviving in any event. Why in God's name are they worried about punishing him?

"You guys are fools!" Yes, I scream at the television. You should hear me when the news comes on.

It's only now that I realize director James Cameron, by adding these fictitious details to the true story, managed to capture a deep, universal truth about humanity's Achilles heel—that we are so subject to irrational emotions we'll waste precious time and resources in seeking vengeance rather than trying to save ourselves.

We *know* the climate crisis is escalating rapidly. We *know* we should focus on "lowering the lifeboats." We know we should work quickly to save as many people as we can, *especially* our loved ones.

But instead we waste our time shooting at generals we don't like, handcuffing immigrants we think are trash, worrying about our missing jewelry. We waste time seeking revenge, no matter the risk to ourselves, to our property, and to everything else.

"Don't you understand?" Rose asks her mother. "There aren't enough lifeboats. Half the people on this ship are going to drown!"

Her mother is unfazed. "Not the better half," she says coolly.

And her coldness is symbolic of what did finally kill over 1500 people that terrible night. Only a handful drowned. The rest froze to death, their lungs free of water as they bobbed along the surface in their useless life jackets.

But the true story of the *Titanic* tells us another universal truth about the state of humanity: even some of the most privileged people on the face of the Earth went down with the ship. Their riches couldn't save them.

The events recounted in the film demonstrate what *not* to do in an extraordinary crisis. And fortunately, there's one key difference between the fate of the passengers on that luxurious liner and the inhabitants of our planet.

We have a chance to patch the leak in time to avoid sinking to the bottom of the ocean.

But we won't be able to do it if we waste time screaming at each other, chasing each other with guns, handcuffing one another to the bowels of the ship as the water rises.

If we can't manage to stop hating the people we hate, can we at least *postpone* our hatred? Postpone our revenge?

*After* we save the ship, *then* let's worry about getting even with all the people on our enemies list.

But for God's sake, let's put our guns away and grab a bucket and whatever other tools and materials we can to stop the loss of the most extravagant civilization the world has ever known.

# Mormons Must Divest from Fossil Fuels

Of the 1145 organizations around the world that have already divested from fossil fuels, 28% of them are religious institutions. But the LDS Church isn't one of them. 15% are educational institutions. But neither the University of Utah nor Brigham Young University are among them. 14% are governmental entities. But neither Salt Lake City nor the state of Utah are among them.

As an essential part of addressing the climate crisis, the LDS Church and every other entity in Utah must divest from fossil fuels.

To ensure a climate in which humans can thrive, we must cut off financing for all new fossil fuel projects, things like storage facilities, pipelines, new wells—any type of infrastructure that would support new or additional fossil fuel extraction and promotion. Many institutions invest funds in fossil fuel corporations, but we must encourage those in our communities to invest their funds in other projects that don't directly exacerbate global warming.

Trinity College in Dublin, the University of Glasgow in Scotland, and the University of Hawaii here in the US are just a few of the educational institutions around the world that believe ensuring a habitable world for their graduates is as important as teaching them career skills. We must encourage leaders at the University of Utah and Brigham Young

University that a crucial part of their responsibility toward their students is to stop funding corporations and projects that intensify our climate disaster.

Worldwide, organizations have already divested over 11.5 trillion dollars from fossil fuels.

We need to pressure businesses and local governments to transition both quickly and justly to 100% renewable energy, which includes retraining of displaced workers. The British Medical Association, Canadian Medical Association, Chicago Medical Society, and New Zealand Nurses Organisation have divested. All of Ireland has divested. The cities of Amherst (MA), Ann Arbor (MI), Boulder (CO), Ithaca (NY), San Francisco (CA), Santa Fe (NM), Madison (WI), Minneapolis (MN), Kansas City (MO), Portland (OR), and New York City (NY) are just some of the city governments that have divested. The cities of Copenhagen, Oslo, Paris, Sydney, Oxford, Stockholm, Cape Town, and Montreal are some others. Can we encourage Salt Lake City to join the list of world leaders?

Thirteen banks in the U.S., Sweden, Germany, France, Austria, Switzerland, and Australia have divested. And a fourteenth bank, the European Investment Bank—the world's largest development bank—has just committed to divestment over the next two years. Can we get some local banks, perhaps Zions Bank, to join the growing number of financial institutions whose leaders understand transitioning to renewables is a sound financial decision?

Organizations like Go Fossil Free (part of 350.org), Oil Change, and many others can direct us in our efforts to campaign, pressure, and encourage powerful institutions to divest. If we don't have the time or temperament to conduct such campaigns ourselves, we can at least donate so that others can.

The Mormon Church insists it will never weigh in on political issues. But it *will* intervene in moral ones. And the climate crisis is a moral issue affecting virtually every life form on the planet. Of course, climate action *is* unfortunately a political issue as well, and it's a scientific issue, a health issue, an issue of self-preservation.

Climate change is an issue of life and death for people around the world, including Mormons.

Many organizations don't like being told what to do. And no organization wants to disturb its traditional sources of income. Successfully pressuring our local governments, religions, and businesses to divest may take some time. But we can immediately start divesting personally on our own.

Mormon scriptures encourage us to always be "anxiously engaged in a good cause." We're told that only a slothful and unwise servant must be commanded in all things. We can each make the decision to divest without a commandment from either Church leaders or government officials.

Over 58,000 individuals have already divested 5.2 billion dollars. We *can* make a difference.

We're not Amish. God has not forbidden us from moving past coal or kerosene.

We must let our solar-powered LED shine before the world. Or watch the desert blossom as the tar pit. Let's divest personally and demand that our employers, our religious institutions, our universities, our city, and our state divest as well.

# Choosing Luxury over Climate Solutions

My husband's a contractor and loves to watch some HGTV shows like *House Hunters*, *Love It or List It*, and *Property Virgins*. Because he's also an environmental activist, however, the shows simultaneously drive him crazy. Some of the programs might just as well be called *Privilege in the Face of Climate Disaster*. While couples bicker over whether the en suite bathroom attached to the guest room is large enough, fires rage across the globe, more and more species go extinct, and politicians insist that the best strategy for addressing greenhouse gases is to subsidize fossil fuel corporations.

I've lived in a mobile home. I've lived in apartment where I had to brush ants off when I woke up in the morning, brush off roaches that crawled up me as I shaved, endure rats eating through the thick plastic containers I'd bought to protect my food. I've had roof leaks so severe kitchen cabinets fell off the wall. I've lived in New Orleans without air conditioning, in Seattle without heat. I understand wanting to live in a decent home.

But watching young, first-time home buyers reject a house just because the appliances are the wrong color is like watching Marie Antoinette struggle to choose which of her fabulous coaches she'll board to escape the French Revolution.

It's rather like watching moderate Democrats bicker over the most "realistic" plan to address climate change, "realistic" always meaning decades of further delay. It's like watching Republicans show how smart they are by allocating yet more subsidies for oil companies already earning record profits.

Critics of a Green New Deal complain that drastic measures to address the climate crisis cost too much.

But how much does it cost to lose 15 million acres to wildfire?

How much does it cost to rebuild cities after a massive flood?

How much does it cost to lose 45% of your crop to drought?

How much does it cost to lose 70,000 people in a heat wave?

How much does it cost to process millions of climate crisis refugees?

How much does it cost to survive the world's sixth mass extinction event?

I remember my first summer as a married man, my husband sleeping as far away from me as possible on those sticky, sultry nights. "Don't touch me! It's too hot! Get away from me!" I understand why heat-stressed cattle are refusing to breed.

Critics of governmental action on climate try to convince us that it's up to everyone else as individuals to make personal changes if we're worried about the environment. "Regulations kill business." Of course, *not* having regulations kills people. And plants. And birds. And fish. Over a hundred thousand sheep and cattle burned to death in the recent wildfires in Australia.

Moderates and conservatives point out we've always had fires and droughts, but one doesn't need a great deal of academic training to understand the statistical difference in the tragedies we see occurring more and more frequently around the world.

The other day, I watched a television commercial advertising a luxurious resort on Paradise Island in the Bahamas. Atlantis dominates the 685-acre land area only a few feet above sea level. As the announcer tries to lure people to this wonderland—the best rooms costing $25,000 a night—I'm not sure either he or the viewers rushing to their computers to make reservations appreciate the irony.

With wealth concentrated more and more in the hands of the 1%, the rest of us are not in a financial position to voluntarily make the sacrifices necessary to curb global warming. Businesses and corporations and the government itself must be forced by law and policy to do the job only they can afford to do.

Perhaps Sofia Coppola can remake the story of Marie Antoinette. In the edgy modern version, she can dismissively say of the peasants, "Let them be baked."

Once we transition to renewables like solar, wind, wave, thermal, and anything else we can come up with, we'll be able to maintain a decent standard of living, though consumerism at its present level won't be sustainable for long under any conditions. But now is not the time to be wrinkling our nose in disgust as HGTV hosts show us million-dollar homes that just aren't up to snuff.

Unless we're using the word in its ugliest form.

Listening to one of Eddie Money's greatest hits from my youth, I now see a wasted town in California. "Two Tickets to Paradise" would simply send us to hell. We need a cover band to adapt the song for a contemporary audience. But I'm not sure "Two First-Class Tickets to the Pyrocene" rolls off the tongue easily enough.

And in any event, who needs a ticket? We're already there.

# Problem Deniers vs. Problem Solvers

When I was a teenager in the late 1970s, there was already a great deal of talk about overpopulation, though we'd just passed four billion humans on the planet.

My religious leaders would scoff at suggestions that bringing more babies into the world could be damaging in any way. God wanted us to bring as many babies into the world as we could. A popular Mormon musical of the time had certain characters singing about "Zero Population" to demonstrate how corrupt they were.

And this nonsense about running out of room or resources? Why, the lower forty-eight states in the U.S. alone consisted of 1,996,725,760 acres. Divided by four billion, each person could have half an acre to themselves. A family of four would have two full acres. Plenty of room.

Even as a true believer, I wasn't convinced. If we crammed four billion people into the lower forty-eight states as described, they could only be allotted that much space if there were no schools, no restaurants or hospitals or movie theaters. There'd be no room for churches or temples.

There'd be no room for forests, so there'd be few building materials for those four billion people to construct housing. And since there'd be no room for mines to extract ore or factories to refine it, those homes would be meager indeed. There'd certainly be no shipping materials from elsewhere without room for roads or bridges or trains.

If every family of four had two acres to themselves, would those two acres be in the desert? On a mountaintop? In a swamp? In a volcanic crater?

Whether or not the Earth could sustain four billion people, or eight billion, or twelve billion, using such ridiculous statistics suggested that the folks making the argument had no clue what they were talking about. When they then added dismissively, "And in reality there's the rest of the world, too," I had to wonder if they were referring to all those acres in the Sahara and Gobi deserts, in Greenland, in Antarctica…

What struck me as even stranger was that the people embracing this delusion acted as if they were describing heaven. Sounded like hell to me.

Who wanted to live in a world where you were trapped for life on two tiny acres, not even allowed to visit friends or family without trespassing on a neighbor's land? Then again, perhaps trespassing wouldn't be a problem since there'd be no police stations or courthouses or prisons. But what happened when your kids grew up and needed two acres of their own? Would they have to move to Canada or Mexico and start gobbling up acres there?

What happened if you had a fourth or fifth child? Would your neighbors have to move farther away to give you more space, forcing *their* neighbors to move farther away, on and on to the border of the nation?

Your kids and grandkids *couldn't* live anywhere close by. All 1,996,725,760 acres were already spoken for.

Often, people who refuse to accept reality will perform extreme mental gymnastics to avoid addressing a crisis. That may get them kudos for their competency in mind games. But deflection doesn't solve problems.

We need problem solvers, not problem deniers.

The first step is acknowledging the problems exist. Too many people on the planet consuming too many resources, and using fossil fuels to do it, meaning even fewer livable areas and resources left for those already here. As hardworking and well-meaning as my Sunday School teachers and other religious leaders were, they weren't up to the challenge.

If we want to solve the problems of overpopulation and climate breakdown, we'll have to think outside the box. That almost certainly means outside the pulpit as well. But whatever the case, that box had better be larger than two acres.

# Cutting Off Our Climate to Spite Our Civilization

We must tackle the climate crisis immediately or we'll lose civilization.

Remember in the movie *National Treasure* when the character played by Diane Kruger discovers ancient scrolls deep under an old church in Manhattan?

"Scrolls from the library at Alexandria," she breathes in awe.

Really? There was a library sticker on the scrolls displaying which branch they came from?

Those kinds of errors in movies bug the crap out of me. But like Diane Kruger's character, I recognize the unfathomable loss the whole world experienced when the library at Alexandria burned in 48 BCE.

I also feel that loss when I think about the fire that destroyed Brazil's National Museum. I feel that loss when I remember how European invaders destroyed every Mayan book they could find. Nazis deliberately destroyed several thousand irreplaceable works of art, and several hundred more were destroyed as a result of bombings from all sides.

Nazis also burned thousands of books. And countless writers and artists.

Over the centuries, many European Americans destroyed as much Native American culture as possible.

The Chinese destroyed tens of thousands of books and music scores during the Cultural Revolution.

Churches and synagogues and mosques and temples have been destroyed by earthquakes and fires and floods and tornadoes. Ancient treasures have been destroyed by fanatics like ISIS. As a global community, we've all lost far too much already.

Yet all of these horrific tragedies *combined* pale in comparison to what modern civilization faces today. This time, however, the culprits are CEOs and shareholders of fossil fuel companies. They're also the workers who drill, who build pipelines, who run storage facilities, who captain tankers, who drive fuel trucks. All of us who allow ourselves to be accessories either before or after the fact are complicit.

In the film *Hotel Mumbai*, we see front desk receptionists at the luxury hotel being forced to help terrorists trick the guests into opening their doors. The receptionists cooperate at first in an attempt to save their own lives, but they soon find the moral burden too heavy and no longer acquiesce, even knowing their refusal will result in their own murder.

A friend of mine who was struggling financially owns land that oil companies wanted to drill. He needed the money and reluctantly agreed to let them. But understanding his contribution to the global climate crisis took a toll on his psyche.

I've been a professional escort. Selling access to my body doesn't begin to compare to the psychological devastation from selling one's soul, even if we're coerced into doing it by an economic system that preys on almost all of us.

Unless we've lived off the grid our entire lives, we're all complicit to one degree or another. And under present circumstances, it may not be possible to stop using or promoting fossil fuels completely.

But we can and must move steadily and *quickly* in that direction.

Planning a trip to Europe? To Disneyworld? Want to buy a new car? A bigger house? A *second* house?

None of these things may be bad, but we're at the point where we need to do something *better*. Let's use that money to add solar panels to our home. We have funds to invest in stocks? Let's put them in companies developing wind turbines. Or carbon capture. Or wave energy. We have options. They need to be ones that limit the coming destruction, not accelerate it.

Unchecked global warming won't stop at destroying a few libraries or art museums. It won't stop at killing a few dozen hotel guests or even wiping out two or three entire cities. The effects of global warming include hundreds of millions of additional immigrants around the world, wars over water, over arable land, over food itself. They include rising sea levels and burning forests and so much more.

It isn't hyperbole to say that the financial stress of transitioning away from fossil fuels is like a single raindrop compared to the financial and cultural torrents that will sweep across the globe if we *don't* transition immediately.

We can cut off our climate to spite our civilization, but the landscape we paint won't be a work of art worth saving.

# The Answer to Climate Denial Can Be Found in Porn

I work in an adult video store, a job that's given me unexpected insight into the motivations of good, religious people willing to continue accelerating global warming no matter how much personal suffering they experience as a result.

Granted, I have other experiences—four years at a Baptist high school, two years as a Mormon missionary, and several years as a Sunday School teacher—which also help me connect the dots, but it's the porn that's offered the biggest revelations.

In the past couple of months, almost *a billion* animals have been killed by the unprecedented wildfires devastating Australia.

Are we trying to create Hell on Earth?

Why, yes, we are.

Most Christians are hoping desperately for the End Times so Jesus will finally come back and usher in a thousand years of peace. We can interpret both the worsening physical and political climate as the long-predicted Tribulation, or we can subconsciously strive to *make sure* these are the Last Days. Then Christ *has* to come back and save us.

Why do some of the faithful nail themselves to crosses on Easter? Why do some believers practice celibacy? Wear hairshirts? Crawl up stairs on their knees? Deny themselves coffee or wine or music? Take vows of poverty? Or do any of the countless other things that add suffering, major or minor, to our lives?

Have you ever been to an adult video store? There are folks who buy a new Squirt video every month, who buy Bondage videos regularly. There are customers into Fisting, into S&M, into Scat.

Yikes.

If there's one lesson I've learned through proselyting for a religiously oppressive organization, it's the cruelty of judging others unfairly.

While I'm not into pain or humiliation, lots of other people are. They enjoy it.

Life is hard under the best of circumstances. If we turn to religion to get through the constant struggle, then religious leaders must give us a viable strategy for coping. Telling us they're powerless to ease our suffering won't do the trick.

But telling us pain is good for us, and encouraging us to embrace it, turns our misery into consensual S&M.

As a missionary, I was kicked and spit on. I had guns pointed at my chest, was threatened with garden shears, was chased down a country road by a driver bent on spraying me again and again with mud. I was stoned with rocks as large as my fist.

It "proved" I was doing the work of the Lord. It validated me.

It also gave me higher esteem in the eyes of my fellow missionaries.

I've had many genuinely happy moments in life—meeting Patricia Nell Warren and Vito Russo, walking the streets of Paris, meditating in the Muir Woods—but I've sure had plenty of unhappy times as well. I watched my mother die horrifically at forty-three. I saw friends die of cancer, AIDS, and gay bashing. I lost my job, my home, and almost everything else in Hurricane Katrina.

We need to give meaning to our suffering or it's just suffering.

One of the regulars at the video store says he can tell that allowing his partner to spit in his face gives the man pleasure, and knowing this gives the customer pleasure, too.

My store also sells Love Cuffs, Pleasure Gags, Enchanted Floggers, and Kissing Paddles.

Many religious fundamentalists oppose anyone trying to end fracking, trying to stop new drilling or additional pipelines. We can *see* the damage fossil fuels do *right now*, but we insist on creating more and more devastation.

Why?

Should we ask the makers of *A Fistful of Submissives*?

We *know* 99% of scientists around the world agree that conditions are deteriorating rapidly. Catastrophic effects don't await us in some vague, undefined future but will drastically change the lives of our youngest grandchildren before they reach high school. Hell, most of *us* will still be alive to suffer new horrors, too.

Paradise, California was merely the tip of the melting ice sheet.

Why in Heaven's name don't we stop what we're doing?

The way some submissives are conditioned to feel they can only "prove their love" by allowing a dominant partner to spank them, religious devotees are often conditioned to believe we can only demonstrate our faith by allowing ourselves to suffer everything "God" inflicts on us until he decides to give us "release."

The Almighty, we tell ourselves, will fix everything *if* he chooses to. He is the Master, she is the Dominatrix, they are the Sadists in control of our spiritual orgasm.

Pain is pleasure for some. But even in consensual suffering, responsible partners establish a safe word.

Here's one the faithful should consider using with fossil fuel corporations and the politicians and religious leaders who support them:

Stop!

# Where Will I Go to Escape Climate Disaster Next Time?

Fifteen years ago, I grabbed my passport, birth certificate, resumé, and my checkbook. Two days before Hurricane Katrina hit, I evacuated my apartment in New Orleans with one suitcase and headed north. I never saw that apartment again.

If being displaced just the one time because of the worsening climate crisis was all I had to face, this might have been no more than a blip on the timeline of my life.

The loss of most of my belongings, while difficult, didn't compare to the loss of my job. I'd been with the New Orleans Public Library for four years when the hurricane struck. I figured that with a civil service job, I was relatively secure. But when your city is devastated…

So I relocated to Seattle and started over. That first winter, we endured a freak rainstorm. Living in a basement apartment on Capitol Hill, I was shocked to find water gushing through the walls, pouring down through the light fixtures. A woman in a nearby neighborhood drowned in her basement, the rising water forcing the door shut so she couldn't escape.

The last few years, though, we've faced Unhealthy and Very Unhealthy and Hazardous air quality from an increasing number of wildfires, smoke so thick I might think I was witnessing a foggy French Quarter morning. Except that I'm inhaling toxic air that stings my eyes and leaves me feeling constant heartburn, even when I'm wearing my COVID mask.

I wonder how much longer I'll be able to enjoy the refuge Seattle afforded me after I lost my hometown. Will I need to relocate again in another year? In two years?

Where will I go?

And how long will I be able to stay there?

How many thousands, or tens of thousands, or millions of other people—Americans *and* refugees from climate disaster in other countries—will be competing for housing and jobs in that next city or country I flee to?

Transitioning away from fossil fuels is difficult and expensive. Carbon capture is, too. So is finding new jobs for folks who must stop earning livelihoods from oil and gas. Transforming our consumer culture to something more sustainable will cause a sense of withdrawal far more severe than anything the pandemic has inflicted on us.

But pretending a hurricane isn't coming won't physically stop the hurricane. Ignoring warnings about the firestorm heading over the ridge doesn't put out the flames.

Governor Inslee ran for president as the climate candidate but couldn't muster enough votes to stay in the race through the first primary.

Neither Senators Murray nor Cantwell support a ban on fracking. Both accept campaign donations from fossil fuel corporations.

Some of our U.S. representatives and state legislators, fortunately, do refuse such campaign donations, but many more do not.

We can invest in Amazon and Boeing and Costco, but we can't seem to invest adequately in wave and thermal energy. We aren't able to retrofit our buildings with solar panels and cisterns. We're unable even to insist that these minimal improvements be required in new construction.

Sooner or later, I'll be forced to relocate. And so will a good many others in the Pacific Northwest.

But where will we go? The West Coast is burning. Siberia is burning. The Amazon is burning. Australia is burning.

The hurricane season seems to grow longer every year and, with steering currents weakening, even Category 1 storms are causing widespread destruction.

I had to travel 2600 miles to relocate the last time. How far will I need to go to find safety the next?

And what happens when there are so many of us that other countries are forced to put U.S. refugees in detention camps at their border?

It's hard to wake up and smell the Starbucks when we smell ash and soot instead.

Let's do something about it while we still can.

# The LDS Church Should Create Solar and Wind Farms

If there's one thing the LDS Church is good at, it's acquiring real estate. Critics find this near obsession less than Christlike, but Church leaders can transform what's currently an unflattering perception into both a financial *and* PR win. The Church can convert some of its agricultural farms and cattle ranches to solar and wind farms to lessen the impact of the climate crisis. By doing so, the Church will also create more outdoor jobs, a necessity for the foreseeable future as we adapt to the new reality of social distancing in the midst of a global pandemic.

Because the LDS Church is tight-lipped about its assets, it's difficult to know exactly how many farms and ranches it owns and operates. Different sources list 290,000 acres in one part of Florida, another 380,000 acres in another part. One source lists 200,000 acres along the Utah/Wyoming border, a tract of 288,000 acres in Nebraska, and various other farms in Canada, Argentina, Brazil, and Zimbabwe. It might be easier for Church leaders to offer transparency, an act that in itself would produce good PR, if they also revealed the contributions they're making toward generating renewable energy.

The Church could hold on to its ranches and agricultural farms suffering under changing climate conditions. Or they could sell them. But they could also convert some of them to solar and wind farms. Many farmers around the world have started combining traditional crops with solar panels, sometimes even using the panels as shade for those crops vulnerable to increasing temperatures. And there's a growing variety in types of wind turbines. The Church can continue to grow crops and raise livestock where appropriate, but it can also generate and sell power to local communities.

The Church gets money. Or it can donate energy to local communities and count that as a charitable gift.

The Church reduces the community's carbon output.

The Church creates more outdoor employment.

The Church gets positive news coverage.

The Evangelical Church in Central Germany generates all the energy its various congregations need—roughly 57 million kilowatt hours—through its own wind turbines. The oldest Presbyterian church in Cleveland, Ohio, doesn't want a turbine to mar its classic 1820 structure but does purchase its energy from a nearby wind farm. In the UK, a hundred Quaker meetinghouses have embraced renewable energy sources, as have another 900 Salvation Army buildings, over 2000 Catholic parishes, and many buildings owned by the Church of England.

The roof of a single synagogue, Temple Beth El in Stamford, Connecticut, generates over 237,000 kilowatt hours of energy a year. There are solar panel and wind turbine companies that specialize in meeting the needs of religious structures.

The LDS Church claims its multi-billion-dollar portfolios are preparation for hard times. Investing to create more outdoor jobs would help address both immediate and long-term needs in the face of the pandemic.

And since even more hard times will increasingly be related to climate change, why not add investments in solar and wind power to Church portfolios? Why not add carbon capture technologies? These and other "green" enterprises are where future income lies, not fossil fuels.

The Church can also invest in geothermal power and wave energy. It can add solar panels to some of their chapels. A solitary wind turbine on every Church property could become as much of a signature as Moroni atop LDS temples.

All these actions would add to global efforts at tackling the climate crisis, making them essential *regardless* of public perception. But they'll *also* create goodwill.

Each president of the Church wants to leave a personal legacy. David O. McKay is known for bringing the 19th century Church into the 20th century. Spencer W. Kimball is known for greatly expanding the missionary program. Gordon B. Hinckley is known for his great strides in reducing societal stigma surrounding the Church.

President Nelson can be known for changing the name of the Mormon Tabernacle Choir. Or he can be known for being the tech president, for bringing the Church into the 21st century and leading the worldwide religious efforts to address our ever more desperate climate emergency, which threatens more lives and livelihoods than even the worst-case projections for the coronavirus outbreak. And that's a lot.

By their fruits ye shall know them.

Let's pray for some climate-friendly fruit.

# I Hope They Call Me on a Thermal Mission

As I watched entire planeloads of Mormon missionaries returning early, I wondered aloud to my RM husband, "How is Church culture going to handle losing this rite of passage?" Record numbers of young men have already been returning home early these past few years, more and more choosing not to serve a mission at all. Anecdotal evidence (the only evidence available given the Church's secrecy) suggests members in general have been leaving the Church "in droves."

But perhaps there's a way the Church can survive both the coronavirus and the abundance of information easily accessible via the internet.

The LDS Church has a long history of accomplishing incredible feats, from the settling of the intermountain west to photographing genealogical records across the world to sending out tens of thousands of volunteer missionaries every year. During the COVID-19 pandemic, the Mormon Church can use its organizational skills and devoted membership to help society transition away from fossil fuels by calling young men and women to serve as "renewable energy missionaries."

We've already shown we can make tremendous changes almost overnight. No more General Conference gatherings, no more weekly church meetings, no more early morning Seminary, no more temple work.

But committed members of the Church still want to serve, and Church leaders can channel that energy and dedication in other positive directions. Since the climate crisis threatens more death and destruction than even worst-case scenarios for the coronavirus, we have no choice but to transition toward renewables.

And since the Church cannot send missionaries on proselyting missions anytime soon, the Church, the members, and the world can all benefit from calling members to transform Church ranches and agricultural farms into wind, solar, and even thermal energy farms.

In the long history of Mormon missionary work, we've adapted many times already. We've sent men into the world "without purse or scrip," sent men on three-year missions, sent missionaries out with no language training, sent women out as well, changed the age for missionary service, sent out married couples, sent missionaries to construct chapels, sent out "health" missionaries, sent missionaries out to do a wide variety of tasks apart from proselyting.

For the foreseeable future, we'll need more outdoor employment. The Church can acquire thousands of hours of labor from volunteers to help defray the cost of the necessary energy conversion. This type of missionary work will also teach young people job skills they'll need after the global recession we're likely to experience. Calling members on renewable energy missions is a victory on every level.

Older folks who wish to serve, or younger folks with physical limitations, can still do so by handling supply orders or monitoring information or performing other functions that don't require heavier physical labor.

And some missionaries, of course, can still serve online missions. Perhaps even these renewable energy missionaries can spend one day a week proselyting online. Others can sharpen their persuasive skills and then petition state and federal governments to do their part in helping society transition to renewables.

Proselyting missionaries are essentially lobbyists anyway. The Missionary Training Center's teaching program won't require much adaptation at all—other than a shift to more online learning. There's much work to be done by a volunteer missionary workforce, all of which benefits the Church and its members both now and in the future.

I served two years as a missionary forty years ago. It remains one of the most profound experiences of my life more than three decades after I left the Church. I belong to a Facebook group for those who served under my mission president, and I'm astounded that several of the young men and women I didn't expect to remain active more than a few months after they returned home are *still* devout members all these years later.

Missionary work can bring converts to the Church, but that's not its only function. It also helps young men and women take an active, meaningful part in what they perceive as a noble endeavor. They work hard, they sacrifice, and they are permanently changed by the process.

If Church leaders want their young people to stay committed to the organization, they need to begin offering something genuinely useful that can counterbalance the secularization of society and the unrelenting availability of unexpurgated Church history online.

Door to door, in-person missionary work will not be feasible for quite some time and might be doomed even apart from the current pandemic. But the Church can still serve its members and the rest of the world by channeling the devotion and goodwill of its missionaries into helping society transition to renewables, an evolution we *must* make in the next few years regardless.

Mormons pride themselves on being the same in every congregation around the world. We teach the same lessons, sing the same hymns, read the same scriptures, believe the same doctrine.

But Mormons also have two centuries of major adaptation. Moving from New York to Pennsylvania to Ohio to Missouri to Illinois to Utah, transitioning from monogamy to polygamy to monogamy, even transitioning from hiding the history of the First Vision to becoming more transparent.

We can do this.

Let's start calling members to serve renewable energy missions.

# We Can't *Eliminate* Our Impact on Climate, but We *Can* Lessen It

Some climate activists grow discouraged when they discover that wind, solar, wave, and thermal energy technologies each carry their own damaging limitations. But that's no reason to give up on renewables. The only way to completely eliminate the negative consequences of human activity on the planet…is to eliminate humans. Short of that, the best we can do is reduce the damage. A transition away from fossil fuels is an essential step forward.

Harm reduction is a term describing the effort to help those addicted to drugs without expecting to solve the problem. For instance, while it's better if a person stops shooting up altogether, if that's not feasible simply by hoping or praying—or punishing—then the next best thing is to make shooting up less destructive.

We provide clean needles and a "safe" place to inject, perhaps have someone nearby ready with naloxone. It's not ideal, but if we can reduce some of the worst consequences of addiction, we have a better chance at reaching the most vulnerable and eventually finding better solutions.

Michael Moore's film *Planet of the Humans* suggests technology isn't an answer to the climate crisis. We must instead significantly decrease the global population and live in harmony with nature. Is the solution then to bioengineer a more powerful disease than COVID-19? Carbon emissions had begun rising significantly even by the year 1900, when there were fewer than two billion people on the planet.

I *hope* it would be difficult to rally people behind killing four or five billion of their fellow man. Even if all 7.7 billion of us here today gave up technology, we'd *still* create havoc with the environment. It would be a different type of damage, and maybe a lesser one in regard to carbon, but we'd still leave our mark, and it wouldn't be pretty.

Remember how the fields at Woodstock looked in 1969?

All other things being equal, what's better for a forest? Cutting down twenty-four trees or three hundred and sixty-two?

What's a better outcome for a nuclear war? Three destroyed cities or seven hundred?

Would you rather your hometown suffer a 5.1 magnitude earthquake or an 8.4?

A simplified example of chaos theory is the butterfly flapping its wings in China and then through a series of unpredictable cause and effect repercussions, it rains in France. The truth is we're *going* to have a negative impact on the environment and climate.

We *can*, though, mitigate the damage. That mitigation will inevitably cause unexpected damage itself, and we'll need to find a way to lessen that. Then *that* mitigation will need tweaking as well. But we don't give up making improvements just because the next step forward isn't 100% perfect.

Perhaps we can't stop the impact of all fossil fuel extraction already in process, but we can certainly refuse to add to the problem. When our frying pan catches fire while we're cooking dinner, we don't pour a bottle of vegetable oil on it to douse the flames. We don't pour water, either. But there *are* options to limit the damage.

We must immediately stop making the worst climate choices possible—oil, coal, fracking, even nuclear with its radioactive waste and potential for sabotage.

Do we refuse to support renewable energy technology because it's developed and sold by corporations? Waiting until the U.S. and other capitalist countries convert to socialism before we begin a full-fledged transition away from fossil fuels is suicide. Yes, it may take such a conversion to repair the worst damage, but we can't wait until conditions are perfect before we act.

We certainly can't wait a hundred years for a global one-child policy to reduce the human population to a healthier level, as essential as that may be in an overall plan.

Our best options at the moment for reducing the catastrophic impact of our presence on the planet are wind, solar, wave, and thermal energy technologies. But even if we completely convert the entire globe to these renewables in the next ten years, that will hardly be the end of human progress. Technology didn't stop with the invention of the wheel or the discovery of fire. It didn't end with pulleys or levers or the steam engine. And it won't stop when we transition away from fossil fuels.

This adaptation *cannot possibly* be perfect. Neither will the next one or the one after that.

None of that means it's okay to construct a single new pipeline or drill even one more well.

We can't eliminate greed or stupidity, either, but we'd sure better find a way to lessen their destructive impact.

Or perhaps we *will* choose a massive human death toll, after all. By default.

Harm reduction works for people and it works for climate, too. So let's develop the renewables we can and start reducing harm before we overdose on the status quo.

# Let's Stop Digging Our Own Graves

A Canadian friend of mine complained that indigenous First Nations people kept refusing the jobs and industry offered them, insisting on government "handouts" instead. They should just "get over" their past abuse, he said, assimilate, and get on with life.

My follow-up question was, "What kind of jobs and industry are we talking about?" Most of the industry I see on indigenous lands supports fracking and tar sands operations. Accepting such a job, no matter the salary, is like getting paid to dig your own grave.

We all know about the billions of gallons of water permanently contaminated by fracking. In a climate increasingly plagued by drought, that's no small matter. Most of the toxic chemicals are supposedly injected deep below ground to avoid polluting our drinking water, but the act of injecting water itself is directly responsible for the marked increase in earthquakes as large as 5.8 in every region where fracking takes place. And much of this "safe" drinking water is easily ignitable as it issues from residential taps.

Toxic water and damaging earthquakes aside, carbon-based fuels are the driving force behind the climate crisis. Driving faster is like thinking the solution to creating safer roadways is to speed when you see the stoplight turn yellow.

Fracking also significantly increases emissions of methane, an even more potent greenhouse gas than carbon dioxide.

During World War II, Japanese soldiers often forced Filipino and American prisoners to dig their own graves. In Jim Crow times, white mobs sometimes committed this same atrocity against their black neighbors. Nazis not only forced many Jewish victims to dig their own graves, but they also forced black Allied POWs—and gays and Roma—to do so. Today, ISIS forces some of its victims to dig their own graves, too. It's a popular war crime.

Why would anyone agree to dig their own grave? They *know* what's going to happen when they finish. Why would they agree both to the hard work and the extreme humiliation? Why would they *help* their oppressors murder them?

People do it to buy time. Not time to be rescued. They know that won't happen. And not quality time. They get only a few awful, miserable minutes. But they're minutes of life.

So people of almost every culture, of every socioeconomic level, in conflict after conflict, agree to dig their own graves.

But some indigenous First Nations people refuse to take part in drilling. They and other activists pile barricades on railroad tracks to stop coal trains. Native Americans and other environmentalists are blocking pipeline construction in the Dakotas.

Members of the Puyallup tribe are fighting a liquified natural gas facility in Washington state. Navajo and other concerned Utahns are fighting to prevent mining and drilling on public lands. Still other Utahns are fighting Salt Lake's inland port for aiding the transportation of fossil fuels.

These folks often suffer poverty as a result. They're routinely imprisoned for protesting.

But they don't dig their own graves.

In her Emmy acceptance speech, actress Alex Borstein spoke of her grandmother being led to a pit where she would be shot and dumped along with other Jews during the Holocaust. The woman turned to her guard and asked, "What happens if I step out of line?"

The guard assured her that although he wouldn't have the heart to shoot her, someone else would.

Borstein's grandmother stepped out of line. She survived while everyone else in the group was murdered. "So step out of line, ladies," the actress told the crowd. "Step out of line."

We don't have to accept fracking and oil wells and pipelines. We don't have to dig our own graves, even if we're being paid well to do the job. And we certainly don't have to accept being shamed for choosing life over death.

Corporations driving the climate crisis have forced us all into a global catastrophe. We're scared. We're hungry. Our kids need shelter.

But they don't need the shelter provided by a tombstone or a vault. If it's an atrocity to make us dig our own graves, it's unconscionable to force us to dig those of our children.

We must refuse all new fossil fuel extraction, storage, and transport. We must step out of line if we want a fighting chance at life.

# I'm My Own Grandchild

Almost every day, we hear climate alarmists shouting, "What kind of world are we leaving our children and grandchildren?"

Frankly, I'm baffled when I hear such appeals. As a climate crisis refugee who lost my job and home to the worst hurricane season on record (since surpassed), who relocated across the country to start my life over at the age of forty-four, and who has since been forced to wear N95 masks during increasingly severe fire seasons, I don't see the climate emergency as some vague future threat.

If country/western artists can sing "I'm My Own Grandpa," perhaps climate realists can come up with a song of our own—"I'm My Own Grandchild."

A recent incident hardly measures as a blip on our overheated radar. On June 27, 2021, a peaceful Sunday, the town of Lytton in British Columbia recorded Canada's highest temperature ever, 46.6 degrees C. The previous record had been 45, set in 1937 in Saskatchewan.

On Monday, Lytton broke the all-time record high it had set the day before, with 47.9. On Tuesday, it broke the all-time record high again, with 49.6 C (over 121 degrees F). On Wednesday, Lytton recorded 49.5 C, just a fraction lower.

That evening, the town of Lytton burned down, 90% of the village wiped out in fifteen minutes. There's the all-too familiar video taken from residents fleeing by car, flames along both sides of the road, buildings and vehicles ablaze. One survivor didn't have time to get his aging parents into a car, telling them to lie in a ditch and then covering them as best he could.

They didn't survive.

Neither did *a billion* clams, mussels, and other shellfish, stranded on a blistering hot beach when the tide receded, dead by the time the tide returned.

Year after year, we see raging wildfires across the planet, towns and human lives destroyed, millennia-old sequoias killed, billions of animals wiped out. Fire tornadoes were once so rare that some meteorologists weren't sure they were even real.

What kind of world are we leaving our grandchildren?

What kind of world are we living in *now*?

Many of us recently learned a new term, "wet bulb." Even growing up in New Orleans, oppressed by the heat and humidity, I'd never heard it. In the past, only occasionally would temperature and humidity combine in a way that prevented completely healthy people from regulating their body temperature and dying as a result, without any underlying conditions, even while sitting in the shade.

But those conditions are developing more frequently in more places year after year.

In the terrible heatwaves of 2003 and 2010, when over 100,000 people died across Europe and Russia, the high temperature was mostly in the mid-80s. But because of wet bulb conditions, it was enough to create massive human death.

Did rising sea levels and encroaching salt water contribute to the Surfside condo collapse in Florida that killed ninety-eight people? It's still too early to say in this specific case, but compromised building integrity on a massive scale certainly *will* happen in the coming years.

Climate change doesn't just threaten tiny rural towns anymore. It also threatens the future of Chicago, Venice, Mumbai, and New York. Several years ago, Indonesia began moving its capital from Jakarta to Kalimantan, in part because of climate change. Global warming has brought Lake Mead to its lowest level since its creation, water that's needed to irrigate millions of acres of farmland. And provide drinking water to twenty-five million people in California, Nevada, Arizona, and Mexico.

Hurricanes, stalling longer and more often because of air currents weakened by climate change, are dropping a year's worth of rain in just a few days on Texas, the Carolinas, and elsewhere. Damage caused by more frequent climate disasters has cost the U.S. over $2 trillion already.

Meanwhile, misuse of groundwater is destroying aquifers around the world, a climate crisis in itself apart from greenhouse gases. A global rise in drought is stressing nations across the planet. If we think the immigration crisis at the U.S. border or throughout Europe is bad now, and it is, hundreds of millions more climate change refugees will soon overwhelm any country left reasonably stable in the midst of increasing disasters.

The unprecedented heat in the Pacific Northwest this year reminds me that even relocating 2600 miles from the last climate disaster I experienced won't spare me. Local crops were destroyed from the heat and trees are dying both from lack of water and because the drought has sparked the release of previously unknown fungi.

What was a surprisingly healthy snowpack in February melted away in just a few days, and at least 194 people died in Oregon and Washington, more than three times the number killed when Mt. St. Helens erupted in 1980.

It's not the end of the world, but horrific climate effects aren't a "distant possibility," either.

This also isn't a "new normal" we simply need to get used to. Next year will almost certainly be worse, and the year after that, and each succeeding year, with minor fluctuations unable to mask a clear trend.

We run the risk of "exaggerating" if we say the climate emergency is happening to *us* now. But we run a far greater risk if we keep pretending it's not happening right before our eyes.

# Every Newscast Must Discuss Climate

As David Sirota pointed out in a recent interview on MSNBC, an occasional mention of climate change isn't enough to reflect the seriousness of the crisis. We need discussion of climate in every single newscast.

When I visited my grandparents as a child, I was fascinated by their obsession with the weather. They only received two stations in rural Mississippi, both a bit fuzzy. They'd tune in first to Channel 3, which delivered the weather forecast at 6:18. Then they'd switch to Channel 12, which delivered the forecast at 6:23.

My grandparents were farmers and wanted to be doubly sure they knew what to expect in the coming hours.

Another early memory is wondering why so much airtime was wasted on sports. There was a war in Vietnam, Watergate trials in Washington, long lines at the gas station. And we needed to spend a full quarter of every newscast on games?

Of course, sports was followed by millions of viewers and brought in hundreds of millions of dollars. It was "newsworthy."

Until climate catastrophe and the world's sixth mass extinction event are treated as comparable to the latest basketball game, we have no hope of adapting to the changes we're already facing.

Wildfires burn entire towns, increasingly severe storms and more frequent flooding events cost more and more each year.

When my grandparents watched two weather forecasts, it was for confirmation or to understand slight variations. It wasn't to get "both sides" on the coming hailstorm or overnight freeze. They didn't see one forecast for a 10% chance of rain and another for a 90% chance and then decide which forecast they were going to believe before deciding to bale hay. All forecasts were based on the best science available at the time.

Of course, given the facts, it might be depressing to spend five minutes of every newscast on climate. And climate news can be scary.

As if news about rising fascism and the decline of our democracy isn't?

Would a news anchor start her broadcast with, "Ten homes in the northeast part of the city collapsed into a sinkhole this afternoon. We'll be bringing you a special report next week at 11:00"?

Crises are newsworthy *right now.*

Ongoing crises like the embassy takeover in Tehran or the Great Recession or the pandemic get covered in every single newscast.

Greta Thunberg points out that we need to treat the climate crisis as if our house is on fire.

If corporations and the wealthy control politicians, and politicians control policy, then the only way to create change is to show people the importance of climate by setting aside part of every newscast, local and national, to cover the crisis.

Of course, since all major news networks are corporate themselves, and since they receive ad revenue from fossil fuel corporations, we must pressure the networks.

But we can't just *wait* for them to do their job. And we can't just complain when they don't do it. The job needs to be done, and while we pressure, we must simply do the job ourselves as best we can.

Whether we're making movies about climate to force the conversation, or writing books, holding rallies, boycotting, speaking with our elected officials, commenting publicly in city council meetings, or whatever else our circumstances allow, we must include climate in everything we do.

Sending a winter holiday card featuring a snowy landscape to friends and family? Include a note about rising global temperatures. Sending congratulations to a loved one on the birth of their child? Include a note expressing your sincere wish that society takes the climate crisis seriously so the child will have a habitable world to live in.

I buy blank greeting cards with photos of fossils or paintings of dinosaurs for just this purpose.

Am I a sick fuck?

Perhaps, but to paraphrase Jennifer Lawrence's character in *Don't Look Up*, "We're all gonna die!"

My country-raised mom shouted this every time we merged onto the freeway, so it comes naturally to me.

We can be kind, and funny, and friendly, *and* insist that climate is important enough to include in every conversation.

When a coworker mentioned cities where she might like to relocate in five years, I said, "Oh, those are great choices. But do remember that the Thwaites glacier will probably have melted by then and that sea levels may have risen a meter. And don't forget which areas seem most likely to be hit with expanding desertification or heavier rainfalls."

Am I a killjoy?

Is covering the pandemic in newscasts a buzzkill?

The answer may well be yes in both cases, but just because we don't *want* to talk about these things doesn't mean we don't *need* to.

If society is going to mobilize enough to address the climate crisis in any meaningful way, the topic must be important enough to speak about for at least five minutes in each newscast. And until that happens, it's up to us to keep it in the minds of our friends, families, and coworkers.

And in our own minds.

We all need to escape once in a while, and we all need a balanced life in order to sustain mental health.

But denial as our primary strategy isn't healthy. That's true when the issue is disease or fascism or corporate influence or climate disaster.

And if we can't make mainstream news cover the climate adequately, let's stop supporting them and instead support independent news that does cover the stories we need to hear.

# Climate Inaction in Action

"9-1-1. What is your emergency?"

"A wildfire is heading straight for our house!"

"Are you in immediate danger?"

"Well…yes! The fire's heading this way!"

"How far off are the flames? How long before they reach you?"

"I don't know. We've never had a wildfire here before!"

"I can only help if you let me. Can you at least guesstimate?"

"For Pete's sake!"

"Is that your final answer?"

"With the distance and topography, I'd say…maybe two or three hours."

"Excellent."

"Excellent!?"

"You seem to have plenty of time to evacuate."

"But there are only two ways out. One is already blocked by flames!"

"And the other?"

"I can't tell from here. The fire could get there before we do."

"But you're not sure?"

"Send us some help!"

"Please calm down. Getting hysterical is counterproductive."

"Oh my God."

"Yes, there is power in prayer."

"Can you *please* send some firefighters?"

"Firefighters and equipment cost a lot of money."

"I pay my taxes!"

"But the CEOs in town don't."

"Just send what you can, okay?"

"Those fire engines burn a lot of fossil fuel, you know."

"I…I…"

"Oh, stop making such a fuss. You haven't even *tried* evacuating yet."

"I don't want to lose my home and everything in it!"

"Good grief. Losing your house isn't the end of the world."

*"Help us!"*

"Okay, okay. Listen, do you have a sprinkler system in your yard?"

"Yes…"

"Excellent. Turn it on."

"We're in a drought. The timer is controlled by the city council. We get half an hour of water twice a week."

"Hmm. I passed the golf course on my way to work this morning. It looked green enough."

"Can you activate our sprinklers from your location?"

"I'm afraid not. But how about this? I can make a call to the city council—an urgent call, tell them it's a priority—and ask them to raise your water allowance."

"What!?"

"Sure. We'll get you *four* days of sprinkler usage a week and increase your allotment to an hour each time."

"Are you out of your friggin' mind!? The fire will be here in two hours!"

"Don't exaggerate. You already said it could take up to three hours."

"We need help *now*!"

"I'm calling the city council on another line as we speak. I'll get them to turn on your sprinklers before the end of the workday."

"Today's Saturday."

"I'll leave a message *and* send an email."

"I…I…"

"No need to thank me. This is what we're trained for."

"Please…"

"I'll put the subject line in all caps."

"Can. You. Please. Send. Some. Firefighters!?"

"Don't you worry. I'll call the After Hours line, too, while I stay on this line with you. You won't be alone. And your sprinklers will be on again before you know it. Plus, I hear the City is about to sign a new contract for better water service any day now. Better filters and everything."

"But…"

"Oh, someone's picking up. I just need a moment to explain the situation to them."

"Tell them to send helicopters!"

"Ah, it's voice mail."

"Tell them…tell them…"

"You might want to pull your window shades down while you wait. That'll deflect some of the heat. Do you have any white paint around the house?"

"Oh my God! The flames are getting so close! They'll be here in thirty minutes!"

"You *said* you had *hours*."

"For the love of God…"

"Please hold."

# Let's Celebrate Higher Gas Prices

People are being murdered in Ukraine to fulfill the pathological needs of a dictator. We watch as children lie dead beside the road, as apartment buildings are bombed, as old women stumble over rubble trying to escape the shelling with their little dogs.

"How terrible!" we say.

"How awful!"

"Someone should *do* something!"

And then our gas prices start to rise as we cut Russia off from one of its major funding sources.

We *care*, we insist, but not enough to put up with *that*.

It's easy to criticize those complaining as shallow and selfish, and some of them undoubtedly are, but most of us are drowning in blood and oil as it is because our own government is led largely by egocentric oligarchs, too.

Financial advisers often ask, "Are you putting enough away to retire comfortably?"

One of my employers confided his personal worries to me once during his lunch break. "Do you think I can retire on a million dollars?"

I put a whopping $25 aside every two weeks. I'm not going to say how much I have in savings, but it's considerably less than a million dollars.

And I retire in two years, the moment I turn sixty-two.

Well, I'll be *eligible* to retire, which isn't quite the same thing.

Why don't I and millions of others like me not put more into retirement accounts? Why don't we plan better? Do we not understand the ramifications?

It's not unlike the questions climate scientists ask us every day.

We're concerned, obviously, with the bills due *now*. Who has time or energy to worry about a future we can barely imagine?

No one wants to pay more for gas. We don't want to pay more for "greener" food choices. And we don't want to support corporations we know are abusing employees and raping the environment, but we can't afford to shop elsewhere.

Like millions of other Americans, not only do I *not* contribute significantly to my savings, but I'm instead often forced to withdraw funds to cover unexpected bills.

Still, my days as an employee *will* come to an end, whether I have any savings left or not.

We *will* kill bees and other pollinators if we keep using bee-killing pesticides.

We *will* increase global temperatures by 3 degrees Celsius if we keep using fossil fuels.

We *will* as a result face worldwide "retirement" without enough environmental savings to get us through the lean years ahead.

Many retirement experts advise clients like me against taking Social Security too soon. It's better to wait until we're sixty-five or sixty-seven.

So why don't I plan to wait?

Because the recent IPCC reports show that irreversible climate damage might occur before I reach a more appropriate age.

There will soon be no option for any of us to delay facing the consequences of our lack of planning.

On my own, I can't stop climate change by giving up beef or wearing my clothes until they disintegrate. Those kinds of individual efforts amount to a drop of oil in a tanker carrying 8,000,000 gallons. $25 twice a month trying to reach a million dollars in two years.

Any meaningful change must take place on institutional and governmental levels. Religious organizations can commit to installing solar panels on all their roofs. Cities and counties can require building owners to paint any roofs not fitted with solar panels white.

The federal government can ban all new fossil fuel projects. It can invest in solar, wind, wave, algal, thermal, and other types of energy production and storage as well as carbon capture.

It can certainly ban fossil fuels from countries attacking and killing innocent civilians.

One thing we as individuals *can* do, though, is stop bitching about the price of gasoline.

Gas prices will soon be the least of our worries. As any Ukrainian can tell you, any Syrian, any Chechen, any Yemeni, any Lebanese, our normal lives and concerns can change in an instant.

So let's welcome higher gas prices as an opportunity to demand that our leaders—local, state, federal, athletic, network, religious, and food conglomerate—make the institutional changes necessary for all of us to reach a healthy retirement age and have a fighting chance to enjoy it.

# Football Has Fans, Religion Exists, and Climate Change Is Real, Too

When I came out to a straight Mormon friend years ago, he reacted as positively as his cultural background would allow. "I don't understand it," he said, "but then, I don't understand why some people don't like basketball, either. I just accept that it's true."

My friend's reaction is a healthy way of approaching reality most of us could incorporate into our own lives.

I'm a former Mormon who's now atheist. Religion pretty much bores me, at least the way it's practiced much of the time. Yet ignoring religion because it doesn't personally interest me would be a mistake, since religious leaders perverting their influence negatively impact LGBTQ folks like myself, limit women's rights, make the lives of workers more difficult. They also shape cultural attitudes toward climate.

We can't ignore reality if we want to enact meaningful climate policies.

At the risk of offending sports fans, I'm not the least bit interested in soccer or football or baseball or hockey. Not even basketball like my Mormon buddy.

But I know that billions of people worldwide follow sports religiously. Whether or not *I* care about it, whether or not I understand why other people do, the fact remains that sports fandom is real.

Universities devote huge portions of their budget to stadiums and training at the expense of academics. Governments orchestrate slave labor to build arenas. People spend thousands on game tickets, spend their yearly allotted vacation to attend playoffs. Fans even riot and kill over the outcome of these "games."

Sociologists devote their careers to mapping out the causes and effects of these phenomena. Lawmakers step in to mitigate the corrupting influence of gambling. Pastors and rabbis write sermons using sports analogies to persuade their congregants to practice spiritual principles.

Meanwhile, I grumble and groan when I'm forced to board light rail at the end of a tough workday and squeeze in beside hundreds of fans heading to the stadium. What could possibly possess people to waste so much time and energy?

Ignoring the reality of sports culture would be foolish. Yet my attitude toward sports is almost identical to that of millions of people worldwide who can't bring themselves to care about climate disaster. Those of us who do care are mystified by their disinterest, the same way my straight Mormon friend can never understand why I don't follow the Utah Jazz.

We need to individualize approaches to reach our friends and family to show them it's normal not to care about every single thing we do but *also* that their lack of personal interest doesn't alter reality.

If it's not a moral failing to feel disinterest in basketball or numismatics or opera—or politics, for that matter—we must accept the reality that our friends and family who aren't interested in reducing greenhouse gases can still be caring, humane people.

Sometimes, because the issue is so important to us, that's a difficult concept. But we can't make progress without accepting this reality as well.

Granted, another reality is that some people are hemorrhoidal assholes who are completely unreachable. I hope we've already learned to distance ourselves from the trolls in our circle. But not everyone is a sphincter who isn't committed right this very minute to stabilizing our climate.

After all, *we* don't devote our lives to every single vital cause, do we? How many of us risk our lives and jobs fighting for racial equity? Or better representation for the disabled in media? Or tuition-free college and vocational training for every American who wants it?

There are too many important causes for everyone to feel the same on every issue. Sometimes, our friends and family have been deliberately deceived, too easily perhaps, but even that doesn't make us morally superior.

Everyone has believed something incorrect, something damaging, at some point. We progress, we learn, we grow, and just because we're ahead on this one point doesn't mean our friends and family may not be ahead on others. If we believe in our hearts these folks are morally "less than" because they don't instinctively appreciate the severity of the problem, our scorn will come out in every interaction.

We must accept the reality that self-righteousness, even when we're right, damages the climate because it impedes persuasion.

Just as I need to plan my commute around sports traffic, we can help people unconcerned about climate understand they still need to make logistical concessions to its reality. Those concessions almost certainly include a ban on all new fossil fuel projects, perhaps rationing fossil fuels to encourage citizens to adapt to changing infrastructure, even diverting part of the military budget toward subsidizing renewable energy, since climate breakdown is an issue of national security.

People who are disinterested in climate issues don't need to *like* these adaptations. They don't even have to understand them. They simply need to accept reality.

So how do we reach Grandma? If she's a dairy farmer, let's try an analogy about milk production. If she's an accountant, perhaps a ledger sheet would work better. Our other friends and family might respond to analogies for gardening, yoga, *Game of Thrones*, or pottery.

Maybe they're not basketball fans but can't get enough tennis.

Let's find an analogy that meets our loved ones where they are. Because climate change is as real as homosexuality, whether we like it or not.

# A Gastric Bypass for Global Warming

At twenty-five, I weighed 190 pounds. Horrified, I fasted forty days over four months while walking two hours a day and lost fifty pounds, which I kept off for another fifteen years. A success story by almost any measure.

This is where we as a civilization were decades ago as scientists who understood greenhouse gases and the corporate leaders who suppressed their research. The planet's "weight," or temperature, might have been managed at that point and kept under control. Even then, it would have taken a great deal of work, but it was possible.

After I turned forty, the number on my bathroom scale slowly began rising. While I preferred weighing 140, seeing 142 wasn't really a big deal, so I accepted it. I wasn't a kid anymore. Gaining a couple of pounds was natural.

As politicians, as corporate leaders, as voters, we began hearing that we should manage global temperature, but it didn't feel *that* hot, so we decided to worry about it later.

Before long, I weighed 145 pounds. That was still a healthier weight than most of my friends. I still looked good, could still pick up a cute guy when I wanted. Dad bods were "in." Life was great.

A couple of months later, I realized I weighed 147 pounds. But that was only two measly pounds above a perfectly acceptable 145. I'd lost my buffer but was still doing okay. I was sure no one else even noticed.

Denial is a normal human reaction.

As politicians, corporate leaders, and voters, we began noticing a few exceptionally strong storms, some troubling droughts, began recognizing that aquifers were shrinking, but if a crop failed in this state, we could always buy replacement yields from that state. It was annoying, but there was no real need to *worry*.

By the time I reached 180 pounds, course correction was already too daunting to attempt. Sure, I hadn't regained all the weight back, but losing forty pounds a second time was going to require an inordinate amount of dedication and effort, and I had a life to live. I was flying to New York and San Francisco and Paris and Rome. Losing weight would have to wait.

Then my husband got cancer, and all my energy went into taking care of him while working my regular job. Naturally, the weight continued to creep up.

We don't make great decisions when we're stressed.

After my husband died, a hurricane struck and I had to start my life over thousands of miles away. Finding an apartment, getting furniture, starting a new job, and trying to make friends consumed every bit of excess energy. I had no reserves for a weight loss regimen.

Internationally, we've had to deal with wars and invasions and rebellions. We've had to deal with recessions and monopolies and real estate bubbles. We've had earthquakes and tsunamis and pandemics and Reality TV.

And insurrections.

I developed diabetes and tried to cut down on carbs, but that meant increasing fats. The pounds kept piling on. My doctor warned me about heart attacks and strokes. I changed jobs, was laid off, found another job, quit, was unemployed, found yet another job, struggled to pay bills, and slowly got back on my feet.

When I reached 244 pounds, more than a hundred pounds over the weight I'd been when I stopped being careful, I realized I was powerless to make any meaningful change on my own. I needed help. An extreme intervention.

Globally, we're losing entire cities to wildfires, seeing towns wiped off the map in flash floods and mudslides, watching entire states, regions, and countries become deserts. We lose forests to pine beetles, coral reefs to rising acidity, suffer from the spread of mosquito-borne disease.

If we don't do something, the planet is going to suffer a heat stroke. Society will suffocate like a climate migrant in the back of a tractor-trailer.

After purchasing some compression socks and a larger pair of pants, I consulted with my physician and was soon enrolled in a bariatric program, planning for a gastric bypass.

That's major surgery, with serious, lifelong consequences, a risk of internal bleeding, a risk of additional surgery, even a risk of death. But I'd waited so long to address the problem that now only drastic action offered any chance at all of success.

Even "success" would never mean returning to 140 pounds. I'll be lucky to reach 180 after two or three years. With my new stomach the size of a hard-boiled egg, I'll never live a normal life, never eat a normal meal, never have a birthday when I can relax and eat so much as a thin slice of cheesecake followed by a single scoop of ice cream.

Never. Not even once. No matter the occasion. *It won't physically be possible.*

Humans can adapt when we must.

As politicians, as corporate leaders, as activists and advocates, as voters, as human beings, we have some serious decisions to make. Do we accept our planet's temperature obesity and the elevated risk of its disability and death without a fight?

Or do we fight?

The choice isn't only between a lower quality of life or death. There's also a third possibility—a lower quality of life *and* death.

In a best-case scenario, we're talking mitigation, survival. We've waited too long to fully recover. Thriving is no longer on the table. But that doesn't mean we don't still have options.

A gastric bypass for the Earth, combined with a healthy diet and appropriate medication, involves an immediate ban on all fracking and all new fossil fuel projects. It involves promoting public transportation over private vehicles, developing more efficient ways to harness and store wind, solar, wave, thermal, and other energy sources. It probably involves even more controversial measures, like a two-child limit or mass relocation away from doomed cities and regions.

It almost certainly means accepting that capitalism exacerbates rather than alleviates our problems.

Bypass surgery isn't *fun*. No one pretends it is. It won't make us "happy."

It's *necessary*.

Or…we can see just how obese it's possible to become. Some people, after all, have surprisingly good blood pressure even when they weigh 600 pounds.

We can visualize such a future, put an obese filter instead of a cat filter on all our video conference calls. Instead of looking at the world through rose-colored glasses, we can see a future—a *present*—where every individual weighs as much as an entire family.

If that sounds like a horror movie, it's nothing compared to what awaits us if we don't act.

The Earth's climate needs a gastric bypass. Let's accept reality, do an intervention, and get prepped for surgery.

# I'm Spending My Children's Inheritance

Imagine you're fifty-five years old. Not elderly. Not young. But you could have had another twenty or thirty good years ahead. Only you don't. You've just been diagnosed with stage 4, terminal cancer.

As a reasonably moral person, how would you react? How would any of us?

Our decision will determine what we do in the face of devastating climate change.

When I was a child, I was shocked to discover that people facing death didn't suddenly become nicer, more righteous. They were about to meet God, after all. Didn't they at least want to squeeze in a few extra bonus points?

Barring a brain injury from an accident or disease, however, our personalities remain consistent as we near the end.

Some people distribute their favorite possessions before they go to make sure the items end up in the hands of folks who will appreciate them.

Others refuse to leave a will. "I don't care what happens to people after I die," one of my partners told me when he was diagnosed with liver cancer.

As hurtful as those words were, they were still better than what many people are doing now—selling off their family's possessions, stealing from their neighbors, and embezzling the retirement funds of others, just so they can have one last, great, fun party.

They're owners of the Triangle Shirtwaist Factory exiting a burning building while leaving their employees locked inside.

Religious conservatives of many types and corporate Democrats, desperate to enjoy life to the fullest, are taking out massive loans after forging their children's and grandchildren's signatures, almost as if they believe they're casting a magic spell that can stop normal biological processes, as if they think they can cast a spell on God himself.

That's not how any of this works.

When climate activists demand we use nuclear energy instead of fossil fuels, I realize they don't really get it, either. Sure, nuclear energy, despite its natural problems, *might* be a reasonable alternative as we transition, but that technology has one major, inescapable flaw.

It must coexist with humans.

Humans attack and fight. They sabotage and bomb.

Humans scrimp and save on costs. They cut corners.

And humans make unintentional, human mistakes.

We aren't compatible with nuclear facilities, no matter how well meaning 95% of us are.

I'm an old, fat man with multiple medical issues. I don't have an impending death sentence yet. Other than the knowledge that I'm mortal and nearing the end of my time here, even under the best of circumstances.

I've already given away most of my prized possessions, living simply and trying to enjoy whatever time I have left.

I have no children, no grandchildren. I *could* choose not to care about the people still here after I'm gone.

But that would mean changing my personality at this advanced stage of my life. Even if I could, I wouldn't be deliberately trying to become *worse*.

It's clear we must drastically and quickly reduce our use of fossil fuels to avoid the worst effects of climate change. Horrendous consequences are already inevitable because of folks who insist on extending their wild, expensive party as long as they can.

That includes everyone who claims profits are more important than a survivable climate. Everyone who willfully chooses to ignore the thousands of reports proving the problem is a real, existential threat.

We can debate the best ways to move forward but building new projects to extract and burn fossil fuels cannot be on the table.

Imagine we're in the audience of a talk show, and the host excitedly announces a surprise gift for each of us. "*You* get a stage 4 cancer diagnosis, and *you* get a stage 4 cancer diagnosis! *Everyone* gets a stage 4 cancer diagnosis!"

That's the situation we're in. Humans may not go completely extinct, but civilization, even in a best-case scenario, will be lost without immediate action. And we're *not* acting immediately. There are a good many projections that suggest it's already too late to do *anything* to save ourselves.

So we're at the end of our life. What do we do?

We can take an experimental treatment and try to survive—drastic climate action—or we can spend the remainder of our days...how?

Being kind to our friends and family?

Spending our last seconds gouging neighbors for one more dollar of profit?

Perhaps we can slap a bumper sticker on our shiny, brand-new gas guzzler: "I'm spending my children's inheritance!"

The answer to the question of our existential morality depends on what kind of person we are.

So, whatever stage of denial you may be in right now, you'll ultimately have to ask the question. What kind of person are *you*?

# This Isn't the New Normal. These Are the Good Old Days

If we dare turn on the news anymore, we see reports of record heat, flash floods, flash droughts. We see thirty-four million people displaced when a third of their country is inundated by record monsoons. We see reservoirs running dry, fire tornadoes, entire towns wiped off the map by wildfires.

There are as many climate disasters these days as there are mass shootings, and they take an even bigger toll.

"Record" becomes a meaningless term these days when speaking of weather, just as "unprecedented" became years ago when talking about politics.

Some newscasters suggest this is the new normal. But it isn't. *These are the good old days.*

We're tired of hearing about climate change, tired of worrying, tired of unsuccessfully urging elected officials to do anything about it.

But being tired of something doesn't alter reality. I'm tired of injecting myself with insulin twice a day. But if I stop doing it, my A1C will shoot up to 10 or 11. The fact that I'm tired of needles and bruises and lumps doesn't change reality.

I'm tired of going to work at a thankless job. But if I stop working, the interest doesn't stop accruing on my loans. The late fees on unpaid bills won't magically stop piling up.

We're tired of lots of things but being tired doesn't change reality.

Action does.

"It'll cost too much!"

Does complying with building codes cost more than not complying? I suppose it depends on the final tab after we factor in having to rebuild the structure once it collapses, once we factor in the settlements to the families of those who were killed or injured in the collapse. Think of the 59,000 people killed in Turkey and Syria, many in buildings where developers fudged compliance with regulations.

The cost is there, one way or another.

In any event, **price tags don't change reality. Climate disaster doesn't go away just because addressing it is expensive.**

King Midas was granted his deepest wish, for everything he touched to turn to gold. Unfortunately, when his food turned to gold along with everything else, he could no longer eat and starved to death.

In recent weeks, we've heard complaints when activists glue themselves to roads, glue their hands to the frames of paintings in museums, or glue themselves together in a chain around the Speaker's chair inside the House of Commons.

"It's not nice!" "It's disruptive!" "It's just theater!"

Well-behaved activists rarely make history.

Of course, making history isn't the goal. We're trying to ensure there will *be* history.

When I hear complaints such as these, coming from "the left" as much as the right, my response is always the same. "If you have a better idea, no one's stopping you."

Nothing anyone's tried yet has forced a decrease in greenhouse gases. While critics wait for the perfect, polite solution, others are desperately trying anything they can think of. Some of those attempts will be offensive. Some even harmful.

"But please," I tell complainers, "if you know what works, do let us in on the secret!"

The truth is that people don't like it when activists kneel. They don't like it when activists stand up. They don't like it when activists block traffic. They don't like it when activists picket. There's really nothing we can do they'll find acceptable.

Well, perhaps a petition they can ignore.

Our goal isn't to be accepted. Our goal is to force change.

The task ahead feels overwhelming. It's easier to pretend it's not as urgent as we know it really is. Otherwise, we end up battling depression along with everything else. And that's not useful, we tell ourselves, so it's *good* to put it all out of our mind.

Let's imagine, though, we're at home asleep with our family when suddenly, we hear armed men breaking in. It's a home invasion.

We have a gun, but it's secured and unloaded so our youngest children don't accidentally shoot themselves. There's no time now to load.

What do we do?

Are the odds so daunting that we just shrug and give up? Do we hand over our spouse to be murdered? And then our oldest daughter? And then our oldest son? And then the rest of the children, including our newborn? Do we then hand over the dog to be butchered, too?

We don't even know if these armed men are trying to rob us or if they're targeting us for our race or political views. We could "cooperate" with these powerful men and hope for the best. Sometimes, that turns out okay. Maybe we'll "only" be raped or beaten and not killed.

Is that a chance we're willing to take?

Or do we find *some way* to fight back? Do we grab a lamp, a baseball bat? Do we call 9-1-1 and barricade ourselves in our children's bedrooms, ready to fight to the death to protect them? Do we lower our kids out the window even if we're on the second or third floor, to give them a fighting chance with moderate injuries rather than injuries much worse if we do nothing?

Don't we try *something* to save ourselves and our loved ones, even if the odds seem insurmountable?

Perhaps we've followed the escalating crime in our neighborhood and have already built a panic room. Maybe we think we can ride out the home invasion without incurring any personal risks. We'll just keep quiet until the bad guys leave.

But what if the bad guys decide to burn our house down, whether to destroy evidence or simply out of spite, while we're trapped inside with our family?

Can we passively leave our fate in the hands of the worst people imaginable?

Perhaps we don't fight to curb global warming like our lives are on the line because deep down we don't really believe it's serious. Maybe we're closet climate change deniers.

Or perhaps we're just at a loss over how to do something "meaningful."

During WWII, we had Victory Gardens. We all agreed to put blackout curtains on our windows. We rationed.

In war, and sometimes even in peacetime, we institute the draft. We're forced to risk our lives for our country. Even if we claim conscientious objector status, we're required to perform some other kind of necessary, risky work to help the war effort. We don't just get to opt out and go about our lives as we choose while others sacrifice and die, merely because we have some distorted view of personal freedom trumping every other consideration.

Most of us are already convinced "something must be done." But we simply don't know what *we* can do personally.

We read articles and watch videos because we keep hoping that finally, someone will have "the answer."

*But no one has the answer.* **And everyone does.**

So what is it?

Do *anything!*

Do the right thing!

Do the wrong thing!

Brainstorm. Try ten wrong things. Fifteen. Thirty.

Doing nothing can't ever solve the problem, so let's do whatever we can think up, no matter how minor, no matter how silly others think our actions. Do it even if others think we're being counterproductive.

Don't let critics stop us.

If a home intruder comes at us with a knife, do we question our instincts? There may well be a dozen better ways to defend ourselves, but we can only use what we have available, and we have no choice but to do it *immediately*.

There's a time for research and planning, a time for rehearsal. And there's a time for action.

Let's try to make a difference in the climate battle using what *we* have at hand, which includes *our personality* and *our individual circumstances*. Let's try and fail if we must, try and succeed if we can.

Taking action on climate is bigger than embarrassment, bigger than guilt, bigger than shame.

No matter what anyone says, let's decide on something *we* can do, big or small, and let's *do it*.

# Successful Citizens Are the Key to a Successful Nation

Many Americans worry that the U.S. is losing ground to China, Russia, or other rising global powers. We think drilling for more oil or banning immigrants or enacting harsher prison sentences will get us back on top or, at the very least, keep us from slipping further off the winner's podium.

However, those aren't the most effective strategies for making America #1. We can't succeed without making the success of everyday Americans not only "possible" but routine. Here are seven difficult ways for the U.S. to win, and one easy way to lose:

First, we must **reduce income inequality**. A living wage is not a giveaway. By definition, folks are working for it. We must raise the minimum wage so that no one working 40 hours a week lives below the poverty level. We also need a comparable minimum Social Security payment. And there's a great deal of evidence that Universal Basic Income is effective.

Affordable housing must actually be affordable if we are to decrease our growing homeless population.

Many of our most successful corporations are already headquartered elsewhere or have sent a majority of their jobs overseas. When we can only ensure success for the top 1%

of our population, we have no leverage to keep corporations or their jobs—and the funds to pay them—here.

We need **universal healthcare**. Every other industrialized nation in the world, and even a few developing countries, guarantee healthcare to all their citizens. If we want to attract and keep the best minds and talents, healthcare must be part of the incentive package. Dental, vision, and mental healthcare must be included as well. We can't keep a competitive economy when over half a million Americans are forced to declare bankruptcy every year over medical debt.

When the number of Americans affected by crushing medical debt is added to the number of full-time workers living below the poverty level on subsistence wages, we already have a population so heavily burdened we can only continue to slip further away from a leading position in the global economy.

The U.S. must ensure **tuition-free college and vocational training**. Like universal healthcare, free or nearly free postsecondary education is guaranteed by many other countries. Some of the best international students will go elsewhere for their education and then work in those other countries as well. We're creating our own competitors. And we can't even concentrate on developing our homegrown students because millions here simply can't afford our skyrocketing tuition.

Even those who take out student loans are then burdened for twenty or thirty years with debt that prevents them from buying a home, making other consumer purchases, having more children, or making financial investments in their own future. And their future is America's future.

Just as a sports team can't be successful unless its players are given the training and other resources they need, a country that refuses to ensure that its citizens are skilled and educated cannot hope to remain a world leader.

**Universal pre-k and subsidized childcare** are non-negotiable if we want successful adults. Workers don't mysteriously materialize out of nowhere at the age of eighteen, prepared to make America's economy competitive. We must begin by valuing childcare and childhood education. And in a digital economy, for kids to succeed in school, they need free access to high-speed internet.

Is such access a "right"? It doesn't really matter. Full access to high-speed internet is *necessary* if we hope to have a skilled population that can compete on the world stage.

Strong, capable adults come from nurtured, educated children.

**Fare-free public transportation** allows even the poorest folks to get to work and back. It's also essential if we want to address the climate crisis. Those with no transportation or access to childcare may be good stay-at-home parents, but they're certainly not contributing to a successful global economy. They often, however, are forced to depend on public assistance.

It doesn't matter if poverty and dependence are technically our goals if they're still the consistent outcome. If we want workers to get to work, we must make achieving that goal something less than a daily Herculean effort.

We must **decriminalize addiction, provide subsidized rehab, and eliminate private prisons**. The war on drugs has led the U.S. to inflict enormous casualties on its own citizens. Legalizing some recreational drugs and decriminalizing others will save our country hundreds of millions of dollars a year, plus create taxable income. It also allows us to stop deliberately destroying the lives of millions of our citizens, a plus even if it didn't save money, which it does.

Our current system of creating millions of unemployable workers each year with felony convictions ensures increasing poverty—or criminal enterprise as the only viable way to earn money. Destroying our own populace isn't an effective way to compete globally.

The last and arguably most important way to maintain or raise our position is to **tackle the climate crisis head-on**. We must become a global leader in products and services for greener forms of energy. We need to find the most effective, least destructive ways to incorporate wind, solar, thermal, or other methods of extracting and storing energy.

Burying our head in the tar sands won't change reality. *Whichever* country develops the best technology and infrastructure to move us away from fossil fuels, to remove carbon from the atmosphere, and to deal with the no longer preventable changes that are now too late to avoid, *will* be the leader of the world. If that's not us, it will be China or Russia or India or someone else. It won't be—*can't* be—the U.S.

We'll *have* to do it eventually, of course, whether we want to or not, whether we come in last or not, so we may as well make a goal to be the best at it.

There are all sorts of other things we could implement—require all high school graduates to master two foreign languages, require a semester abroad for every college degree, or a year of teaching ESL to immigrants. We could require community service instead of military service and retrofit buildings with energy-efficient windows or solar panels or whatever, teaching marketable skills in the process. There are many other things we could do to improve our country, but we only NEED these seven.

And we'll pay for these things one way or another. Prisons aren't cheap. Neither are riots in response to racism and other forms of oppression. Cleaning up oil spills or water polluted by fracking isn't free. Neither is the destruction caused by longer wildfire and stronger hurricane seasons. Droughts and floods aren't cheap. Neither is relocating coastal communities.

We can divert hundreds of billions from our military budget and still fund at a level four times that of either China or Russia. We can tax corporations and the wealthy at the same levels we did in the 1950s and have more than enough funds to implement these changes.

So what's the **one easy, sure way for America to fail**? Choosing austerity programs. This, of course, can be broken down into smaller pieces—pitting workers against each other, taxing everyone except the rich, cutting back on every form of assistance, trickle-down economics—but it's all basically the same thing. When we structure every benefit to favor the top 1% of citizens and weigh down the other 99%, we ensure with absolute certainty that 99% of our population will not be able to compete effectively with the Chinese or Russians.

Just as it's easier to deface property than to construct it, just as it's easier to burn a book than to write one, it's easier to choose austerity over the difficult programs we'll need to lift our country.

It boils down to this: do we *want* healthy, educated, well-balanced adults? Then we'd better not start two decades after their most formative years. Do we want a skilled, educated, debt-free population capable of competing globally in every major industry? Then we'd better stop throwing up as many barriers as possible. We must accept responsibility for the workforce we do—or don't—create.

None of these winning strategies is easy. But then, no one wins a gold medal by putting off strenuous workouts. No one is named valedictorian for shrugging off chemistry and literature classes. No one wins a Nobel Peace Prize for justifying mass incarceration and extrajudicial killings.

There's only one way to be competitive on the world stage, and that's by making our citizens successful. We don't *have* to do it, of course. We *can* let the inertia of our current poor policies keep dragging us down.

That's certainly the easier path.

But if we want to succeed, we'll need to stop deifying oppression in all its forms. We must change our downward course by telling officials already in office exactly what we demand, and only support those candidates in future elections who are willing to take immediate action.

Sound hard?

Well, you didn't think it would be easy, did you?

So let's get to work.

# Books by Johnny Townsend

Thanks for reading! If you enjoyed this book, could you please take a few minutes to write a review online? Reviews are helpful both to me as an author and to other readers, so we'd all sincerely appreciate your writing one! And if you did enjoy the book, here are some others I've written you might want to look up:

Mormon Underwear

Zombies for Jesus

A Gay Mormon Missionary in Pompeii

The Golem of Rabbi Loew

Marginal Mormons

Sexual Solidarity

The Mysterious Madness of Mormons

Going-Out-Of-Religion Sale

Escape from Zion

Gayrabian Nights

Invasion of the Spirit Snatchers

The Washing of Brains

Sins of the Saints

Mormon Misfits

Gay Gaslighting

Out of the Missionary's Closet

The Last Days Linger

Human Compassion for Beginners

Breaking the Promise of the Promised Land

I Will, Through the Veil

Am I My Planet's Keeper?

Have Your Cum and Eat It, Too

Strangers with Benefits

Constructing Equity

Wake Up and Smell the Missionaries

Racism by Proxy

Orgy at the STD Clinic

Please Evacuate

Recommended Daily Humanity

The Camper Killings

Kinky Quilts: Patchwork Designs for Gay Men

An Eternity of Mirrors: Best Short Stories of Johnny Townsend

Inferno in the French Quarter: The UpStairs Lounge Fire

Latter-Gay Saints: An Anthology of Gay Mormon Fiction (co-editor)

Available from your favorite online or neighborhood bookstore.

Wondering what some of those other books are about? Read on!

**Invasion of the Spirit Snatchers**

During the Apocalypse, a group of Mormon survivors in Hurricane, Utah gather in the home of the Relief Society president, telling stories to pass the time as they ration their food storage and await the Second Coming. But this is no ordinary group of Mormons— or perhaps it is. They are the faithful, feminist, gay, apostate, and repentant, all working together to help each other through the darkest days any of them have yet seen.

## Gayrabian Nights

*Gayrabian Nights* is a twist on the well-known classic, *1001 Arabian Nights*, in which Scheherazade, under the threat of death if she ceases to captivate King Shahryar's attention, enchants him through a series of mysterious, adventurous, and romantic tales.

In this variation, a male escort, invited to the hotel room of a closeted, homophobic Mormon senator, learns that the man is poised to vote on a piece of anti-gay legislation the following morning. To prevent him from sleeping, so that the exhausted senator will miss casting his vote on the Senate floor, the escort entertains him with stories of homophobia, celibacy, mixed orientation marriages, reparative therapy, coming out, first love, gay marriage, and long-term successful gay relationships.

The escort crafts the stories to give the senator a crash course in gay culture and sensibilities, hoping to bring the man closer to accepting his own sexual orientation.

# Inferno in the French Quarter: The UpStairs Lounge Fire

On Gay Pride Day in 1973, someone set the entrance to a French Quarter gay bar on fire. In the terrible inferno that followed, thirty-two people lost their lives, including a third of the local congregation of the Metropolitan Community Church, their pastor burning to death halfway out a second-story window as he tried to claw his way to freedom.

A mother who'd gone to the bar with her two gay sons died alongside them. A man who'd helped his friend escape first was found dead near the fire escape. Two children waited outside a movie theater across town for a father and "uncle" who would never pick them up. During this era of rampant homophobia, several families refused to claim the bodies, and many churches refused to bury the dead.

Author Johnny Townsend pored through old records and tracked down survivors of the fire as well as relatives and friends of those killed to compile this fascinating account of a forgotten moment in gay history.

## A Gay Mormon Missionary in Pompeii

What is a gay Mormon missionary doing in Italy? He is trying to save his own soul as well as the souls of others. In these tales chronicling the two-year mission of Robert Anderson, we see a young man tormented by his inability to be the man the Church says he should be. In addition to his personal hell, Anderson faces a major earthquake, organized crime, a serious bus accident, and much more. He copes with horrendous mission leaders and his own suicidal tendencies. But one day, he meets another missionary who loves him, and his world changes forever.

## The Golem of Rabbi Loew

Jacob and Esau Cohen are the closest of brothers. In fact, they're lovers. A doctor tries to combine canine genes with those of Jews, to improve their chances of surviving a hostile world. A Talmudic scholar dates an escort. A scientist tries to develop the "God spot" in the brains of his patients in hopes of creating a messiah.

A Jew-by-Choice navigates Jewish/Muslim relations during Pesach. A gay Lubavitcher dating a Catholic is attacked and left for dead but becomes a police officer in response. The Golem of Prague is really Rabbi Loew's secret lover.

While some of the Jews in Townsend's book are Orthodox, this collection of Jewish stories most certainly is not.

## Wake Up and Smell the Missionaries

Two Mormon missionaries in Italy discover they share the same rare ability—both can emit pheromones on demand. At first, they playfully compete in the hills of Frascati to see who can tempt "investigators" most. But soon they're targeting each other non-stop.

Can two immature young men learn to control their "superpower" to live a normal life…and develop genuine love? Even as their relationship is threatened by the attentions of another man?

They seem just on the verge of success when a massive earthquake leaves them trapped under the rubble of their apartment in Castellammare.

With night falling and temperatures dropping, can they dig themselves out in time to save themselves? And will their injuries destroy the ability that brought them together in the first place?

## Orgy at the STD Clinic

Todd Tillotson is struggling to move on after his husband is killed in a hit and run attack a year earlier during a Black Lives Matter protest in Seattle.

In this novel set entirely on public transportation, we watch as Todd, isolated throughout the pandemic, battles desperation in his attempt to safely reconnect with the world.

Will he find love again, even casual friendship, or will he simply end up another crazy old man on the bus?

Things don't look good until a man whose face he can't even see sits down beside him despite the raging variants.

And asks him a question that will change his life.

## Please Evacuate

A gay, partygoing New Yorker unconcerned about the future or the unsustainability of capitalism is hit by a truck and thrust into a straight man's body half a continent away. As Hunter tries to figure out what's happening, he's caught up in another disaster, a wildfire sweeping through a Colorado community, the flames overtaking him and several schoolchildren as they flee.

When he awakens, Hunter finds himself in the body of yet another man, this time in northern Italy, a former missionary about to marry a young Mormon woman. Still piecing together this new reality, and beginning to embrace his latest identity, Hunter fights for his life in a devastating flash flood along with his wife *and* his new husband.

He's an aging worker in drought-stricken Texas, a nurse at an assisted living facility in the direct path of a hurricane, an advocate for the unhoused during a freak Seattle blizzard.

We watch as Hunter is plunged into life after life, finally recognizing the futility of only looking out for #1 and understanding the part he must play in addressing the global climate crisis…if he ever gets another chance.

## Recommended Daily Humanity

A checklist of human rights must include basic housing, universal healthcare, equitable funding for public schools, and tuition-free college and vocational training.

In addition to the basics, though, we need much more to fully thrive. Subsidized childcare, universal pre-K, a universal basic income, subsidized high-speed internet, net neutrality, fare-free public transit (plus *more* public transit), and medically assisted death for the terminally ill who want it.

None of this will matter, though, if we neglect to address the rapidly worsening climate crisis.

Sound expensive? It is.

But not as expensive as refusing to implement these changes. The cost of climate disasters each year has grown to staggering figures. And the cost of social and political upheaval from not meeting the needs of suffering workers, families, and individuals may surpass even that.

It's best we understand that the vast sums required to enact meaningful change are an investment which will pay off not only in some indeterminate future but in fact almost immediately. And without these adjustments to our lifestyles and values, there may very well not be a future capable of sustaining freedom and democracy…or even civilization itself.

# The Camper Killings

When a homeless man is found murdered a few blocks from Morgan Beylerian's house in south Seattle, everyone seems to consider the body just so much additional trash to be cleared from the neighborhood. But Morgan liked the guy. They used to chat when Morgan brought Nick groceries once a week.

And the brutal way the man was killed reminds Morgan of their shared Mormon heritage, back when the faithful agreed to have their throats slit if they ever revealed temple secrets.

Did Nick's former wife take action when her ex-husband refused to grant a temple divorce? Did his murder have something to do with the public accusations that brought an end to his promising career?

Morgan does his best to investigate when no one else seems to care, but it isn't easy as a man living paycheck to paycheck himself, only able to pursue his investigation via public transit.

As he continues his search for the killer, Morgan's friends withdraw and his husband threatens to leave. When another homeless man is killed and Morgan is accused of the crime, things look even bleaker.

But his troubles aren't over yet.

Will Morgan find the killer before the killer finds him?

## Mormon Misfits

LGBTQ Mormons may not be a good fit for the LDS world, but there's plenty of room for them elsewhere.

A budding feminist tries to make a political statement by giving birth to her "illegitimate" son in church just before Mother's Day. A gay man works with unhoused people in Seattle while taking care of a terminally ill partner at home. A lesbian couple fight internalized homophobia that has them questioning if their desperate financial situation is a punishment from God. A man trains himself to stop praying. A gay man falls in love in Morocco. Another man learns his boyfriend was at a nightclub when a mass shooter attacked.

Few of us are a perfect fit for the culture we're born into, yet even as religious intolerance makes a desperate comeback attempt, there are good, like-minded folks everywhere. And love always wins in the end.

# Gay Gaslighting

Family members and religious leaders often invoke "love" as their justification for making the lives of LGBTQ folks difficult. But we've learned how to nurture one another.

In these tales from the author of *Mormon Underwear* and *Gayrabian Nights*, a gay man invites two young Mormon missionaries to watch movies on their day off, offering R-rated and eventually X-rated films for their edification. A man receives a substantial inheritance...on the condition he leave his husband. A customer service rep at a Suicide Center established under a new theocracy "assists" those condemned of homosexuality kill themselves.

A bishop is murdered by one of his congregants for being too "liberal." A lonely wife discovers that her husband of twenty-six years is gay. Two missionaries try to interest men at an adult video store in the LDS Church. Parents tell their son he's ugly from the time they first suspect he's gay, hoping he'll be afraid to date once he becomes an adult.

As the fight to remain free of theocracy intensifies, it's important to understand what we're up against and prepare for the political—and emotional—battles ahead. One way is by telling stories oppressors don't want us to hear.

## Sexual Solidarity

"Gay Ex-Mormons Unite!" In these tales by a former Mormon missionary, a polygamist in 1855 Utah is ordered to take a fourth wife, when all he really wants is to be with another man. A Victorian enthusiast has a startling sexual revelation to make at his monthly Society meeting. A gay Mormon hires a hit man in a desperate bid to stop himself from breaking the Law of Chastity.

A Relief Society president is trapped on a plane next to a gay man flaunting his sexuality. The Three Nephites seek counseling to deal with their sexual frustrations since their wives aren't immortal as they are. A worthy gay man becomes a ministering angel in the afterlife. A Mormon missionary in Italy moves in with a man he's been teaching.

Gay men don't always have lots in common, but most of us understand religious bigotry and will enjoy reading some of the many ways we've learned not only to cope but also find *"Sexual Solidarity"* with one another.

# Sins of the Saints

In this collection of stories by ex-Mormon author Johnny Townsend, we see a missionary cope with the startling discovery that his companion has been translated off the face of the Earth. A teenage girl pretends to be her brother so she can "hold the priesthood" for at least a day.

A young man taught that loved ones watch over family members from the Other Side keeps imagining his grandmother catching him masturbating. A former prostitute, now a faithful Latter-day Saint, finds that some of her fellow congregants can't get beyond her past. A schizophrenic Single Adult leads a secret life no one in her congregation suspects.

# The Mysterious Madness of Mormons

When religious indoctrination clashes with reality, the outcome can't always be predicted. In these stories by the author of *Please Evacuate* and *Inferno in the French Quarter*, a Seminary teacher threatens to kill his students. A schizophrenic woman in a hurricane evacuation shelter finds love.

A Relief Society president's silicone breast implants develop into a new life form. A sister missionary suffocating under family pressure volunteers to be held hostage during a bank robbery. A teenage girl is haunted by the ghost of Emma Smith. A devout Mormon takes up sex work to raise money to help the poor.

Sometimes, behavior that seems perfectly reasonable in one culture can seem disturbing to those outside it. But whether reasonable or disturbing, their stories can also make compelling reading.

## Escape from Zion

In these short stories by ex-Mormon author Johnny Townsend, parents hire men to pose as the Three Nephites to teach their children the Book of Mormon is true. A shy single woman meets the man of her dreams at an endoscopy party.

An anti-Mormon mob threatens a church outing. A deceased sinner plots to break out of Spirit Prison. Aliens visiting the UN reveal that God really does live on the planet Kolob. Mormons survive the zombie apocalypse because of their two-year supply of food. A young couple desperately try to escape after America becomes a theocracy.

# What Readers Have Said

Townsend's stories are "a gay *Portnoy's Complaint* of Mormonism. Salacious, sweet, sad, insightful, insulting, religiously ethnic, quirky-faithful, and funny."

D. Michael Quinn, author of *The Mormon Hierarchy: Origins of Power*

"Told from a believably conversational first-person perspective, [*A Gay Mormon Missionary in Pompeii*'s] novelistic focus on Anderson's journey to thoughtful self-acceptance allows for greater character development than often seen in short stories, which makes this well-paced work rich and satisfying, and one of Townsend's strongest. An extremely important contribution to the field of Mormon fiction." Named to Kirkus Reviews' Best of 2011.

*Kirkus Reviews*

"The thirteen stories in *Mormon Underwear* capture this struggle [between Mormonism and homosexuality] with humor, sadness, insight, and sometimes shocking details....*Mormon Underwear* provides compelling stories, literally from the inside-out."

Niki D'Andrea, *Phoenix New Times*

"Townsend's lively writing style and engaging characters [in *Zombies for Jesus*] make for stories which force us to wake up, smell the (prohibited) coffee, and review our attitudes with regard to reading dogma so doggedly. These are tales which revel in the individual tics and quirks which make us human, Mormon or not, gay or not…"

A.J. Kirby, *The Short Review*

"The Rift," from *A Gay Mormon Missionary in Pompeii*, is a "fascinating tale of an untenable situation…a *tour de force*."

David Lenson, editor, *The Massachusetts Review*

"Pronouncing the Apostrophe," from *The Golem of Rabbi Loew*, is "quiet and revealing, an intriguing tale…"

Sima Rabinowitz, Literary Magazine Review, *NewPages.com*

*The Circumcision of God* is "a collection of short stories that consider the imperfect, silenced majority of Mormons, who may in fact be [the Church's] best hope….[The book leaves] readers regretting the church's willingness to marginalize those who best exemplify its ideals: those who love fiercely despite all obstacles, who brave challenges at great personal risk and who always choose the hard, higher road."

*Kirkus Reviews*

In *Mormon Fairy Tales*, Johnny Townsend displays "both a wicked sense of irony and a deep well of compassion."

Kel Munger, *Sacramento News and Review*

*Zombies for Jesus* is "eerie, erotic, and magical."

*Publishers Weekly*

"While [Townsend's] many touching vignettes draw deeply from Mormon mythology, history, spirituality and culture, [*Mormon Fairy Tales*] is neither a gaudy act of proselytism nor angry protest literature from an ex-believer. Like all good fiction, his stories are simply about the joys, the hopes and the sorrows of people."

*Kirkus Reviews*

"In *Inferno in the French Quarter* author Johnny Townsend restores this tragic event [the UpStairs Lounge fire] to its proper place in LGBT history and reminds us that the victims of the blaze were not just 'statistics,' but real people with real lives, families, and friends."

Jesse Monteagudo, *The Bilerico Project*

In *Inferno in the French Quarter*, "Townsend's heart-rending descriptions of the victims…seem to [make them] come alive once more."

Kit Van Cleave, *OutSmart Magazine*

*Marginal Mormons* is "an irreverent, honest look at life outside the mainstream Mormon Church….Throughout his musings on sin and forgiveness, Townsend beautifully demonstrates his characters' internal, perhaps irreconcilable struggles….Rather than anger and disdain, he offers an honest portrayal of people searching for meaning and community in their lives, regardless of their life choices or secrets." Named to Kirkus Reviews' Best of 2012.

*Kirkus Reviews*

The stories in *The Mormon Victorian Society* "register the new openness and confidence of gay life in the age of same-sex marriage….What hasn't changed is Townsend's wry, conversational prose, his subtle evocations of character and social dynamics, and his deadpan humor. His warm empathy still glows in this intimate yet clear-eyed engagement with Mormon theology and folkways. Funny, shrewd and finely wrought dissections of the awkward contradictions—and surprising harmonies—between conscience and desire." Named to Kirkus Reviews' Best of 2013.

*Kirkus Reviews*

"This collection of short stories [*The Mormon Victorian Society*] featuring gay Mormon characters slammed [me] in the face from the first page, wrestled my heart and mind to the floor, and left me panting and wanting more by the end. Johnny Townsend has created so many memorable characters in such few pages. I went weeks thinking about this book. It truly touched me."

Tom Webb, *A Bear on Books*

*Dragons of the Book of Mormon* is an "entertaining collection....Townsend's prose is sharp, clear, and easy to read, and his characters are well rendered..."

*Publishers Weekly*

"The pre-eminent documenter of alternative Mormon lifestyles...Townsend has a deep understanding of his characters, and his limpid prose, dry humor and well-grounded (occasionally magical) realism make their spiritual conundrums both compelling and entertaining. [*Dragons of the Book of Mormon* is] [a]nother of Townsend's critical but affectionate and absorbing tours of Mormon discontent." Named to Kirkus Reviews' Best of 2014.

*Kirkus Reviews*

In *Gayrabian Nights*, "Townsend's prose is always limpid and evocative, and…he finds real drama and emotional depth in the most ordinary of lives."

*Kirkus Reviews*

*Gayrabian Nights* is a "complex revelation of how seriously soul damaging the denial of the true self can be."

Ryan Rhodes, author of *Free Electricity*

*Gayrabian Nights* "was easily the most original book I've read all year. Funny, touching, topical, and thoroughly enjoyable."

*Rainbow Awards*

*Lying for the Lord* is "one of the most gripping books that I've picked up for quite a while. I love the author's writing style, alternately cynical, humorous, biting, scathing, poignant, and touching…. This is the third book of his that I've read, and all are equally engaging. These are stories that need to be told, and the author does it in just the right way."

Heidi Alsop, *Ex-Mormon Foundation Board Member*

In *Lying for the Lord*, Townsend "gets under the skin of his characters to reveal their complexity and conflicts....shrewd, evocative [and] wryly humorous."

*Kirkus Reviews*

In *Missionaries Make the Best Companions*, "the author treats the clash between religious dogma and liberal humanism with vivid realism, sly humor, and subtle feeling as his characters try to figure out their true missions in life. Another of Townsend's rich dissections of Mormon failures and uncertainties..." Named to Kirkus Reviews' Best of 2015.

*Kirkus Reviews*

In *Invasion of the Spirit Snatchers*, "Townsend, a confident and practiced storyteller, skewers the hypocrisies and eccentricities of his characters with precision and affection. The outlandish framing narrative is the most consistent source of shock and humor, but the stories do much to ground the reader in the world—or former world—of the characters....A funny, charming tale about a group of Mormons facing the end of the world."

*Kirkus Reviews*

"Townsend's collection [*The Washing of Brains*] once again displays his limpid, naturalistic prose, skillful narrative chops, and his subtle insights into psychology...Well-crafted dispatches on the clash between religion and self-fulfillment..."

*Kirkus Reviews*

"While the author is generally at his best when working as a satirist, there are some fine, understated touches in these tales [*The Last Days Linger*] that will likely affect readers in subtle ways….readers should come away impressed by the deep empathy he shows for all his characters—even the homophobic ones."

*Kirkus Reviews*

"Written in a conversational style that often uses stories and personal anecdotes to reveal larger truths, this immensely approachable book [*Racism by Proxy*] skillfully serves its intended audience of White readers grappling with complex questions regarding race, history, and identity. The author's frequent references to the Church of Jesus Christ of Latter-day Saints may be too niche for readers unfamiliar with its idiosyncrasies, but Townsend generally strikes a perfect balance of humor, introspection, and reasoned arguments that will engage even skeptical readers."

*Kirkus Reviews*

*Orgy at the STD Clinic* portrays "an all-too real scenario that Townsend skewers to wincingly accurate proportions…[with] instant classic moments courtesy of his punchy, sassy, sexy lead character…"

Jim Piechota, *Bay Area Reporter*

*Orgy at the STD Clinic* is "...a triumph of humane sensibility. A richly textured saga that brilliantly captures the fraying social fabric of contemporary life." Named to Kirkus Reviews' Best Indie Books of 2022.

*Kirkus Reviews*

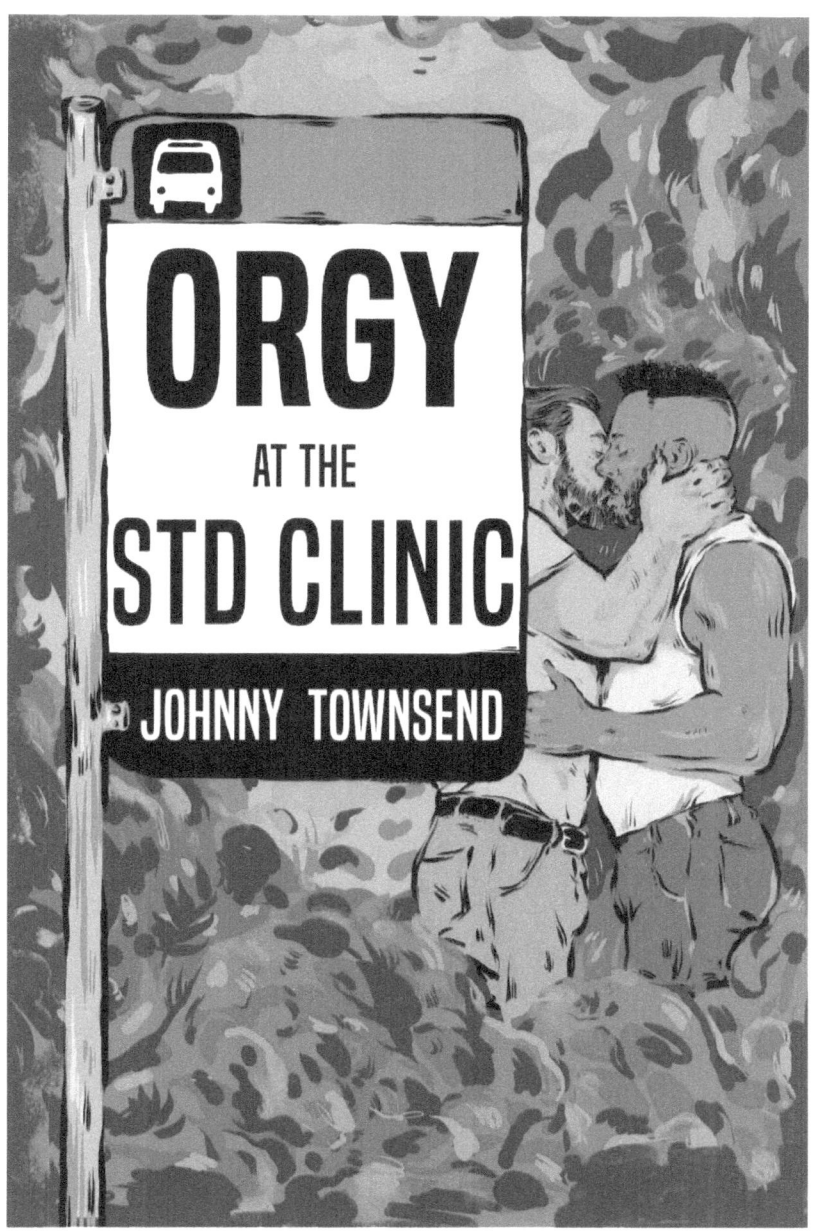

JOHNNY TOWNSEND

ESCAPE
FROM ZION

RECOMMENDED
DAILY
HUMANITY

JOHNNY TOWNSEND